ILLUSTRATED LIBRARY OF COOKING

VOLUME 11 Lun-Nut

*Puzzled about what to put in
a lunch box? Or how to cook a
picnic at home and carry it
to the picnic ground?
Wondering how to plan a
party lunch or brunch?
Looking for unique and nifty
ways to camouflage leftovers
so the family doesn't recognize
them? If you've answered
"yes" to any one question,
you will find Volume 11 a
most welcome friend in need.*

ROCKVILLE HOUSE PUBLISHERS, INC.
ROCKVILLE CENTRE, NEW YORK 11570

Family Circle.

Illustrated Library of

COOKING

YOUR READY REFERENCE FOR A LIFETIME OF GOOD EATING

Way to wow friends—with a lively Italian Festa, served midday as a brunch. Souffléed Seafood Ramekins begin the meal, pepperoni-stuffed Veal Roast Italiano is the entrée.

Table of Contents

THE LUNCH BOX

**THE LUNCH BOX:
TIPS ON PACKING A LUNCH, HOW TO
MAKE A LUNCH BOX OR
BAG APPEALING.**

Today's box and bag lunches are going gourmet. No more dry peanut butter-and-jelly sandwiches or soggy lettuce and tomato. Insulated tote bags and "canned ice" make it possible to pack all of yesterday's unpackables: a lavish lobster salad, for example, a gooey cream-filled French pastry, an exquisitely sauced piece of meat. These foods can now be kept cool in transit and, thanks to sturdy portion-sized plastic containers (available in rounds, squares, rectangles and wedges for pies), they can also be kept neat and fresh and *separate*. No more mayonnaise on the cake, deviled egg on the orange or coffee on the cookies. And no more "squashed" sandwiches or shattered crackers.

Sandwich bags are miracle workers, too, keeping sandwiches fresh and moist and tasting the way they should instead of like carrots or apples or any of their other aromatic traveling companions.

What lunchbox toter wouldn't welcome one of these?

The insulated tote bags that do such a good job of keeping foods cool will also keep foods hot, meaning that a Thermos can be filled with a special soup or stew, a zippy chili, perhaps, or even a favorite curry. Come lunchtime, these foods will be hot and savory, almost as if they had been served straight from the stove.

In the pages that follow, you'll find recipes for a number of original, opulent box lunches, also tips on wrapping and packing. Box lunches, you might say, are "in the bag."

1287

PACKING A LUNCH?
TRY THESE INSIDE TIPS

Pull Some Hocus-Pocus:
With two kinds of bread, sandwiches taste twice as good—and fixing them puts some fun in the job for the chef. Sketches show a few ways to

mix and match the sections. Another hint: For easy handling, cut sandwiches for youngsters in six or eight small wedges.

Keep Extras under Separate Wraps:
To hold lettuce and cucumber crisp and fresh, bundle separately into wet paper toweling, then into wax paper, foil or transparent wrap. Come lunchtime, they're ready to add to a sandwich. Raw nibbles travel neatly in a plastic bag, make packing a snap.

1288

Pamper a Sweet Tooth:
A little imagination turns dessert into a surprise treat and makes lunchtime much more inviting. To keep frosting on a cupcake and off the wrapper, split the cake and put the frosting inside, sandwich style. For apple fans, core the fruit first, then stuff center with a piece of their favorite cheese.

Bow to Weight-Watchers:
Snipping calories? No need to give up a sandwich—just make it open-face, with only one slice of bread. Or skip the bread entirely and layer sliced tomatoes, cottage cheese or crisp pickle chips between two pieces of ham or meat loaf to eat with a fork.

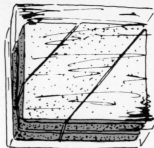

Turn Lunch into a Frozen Asset:
When time's short, a complete meal, already packed and tucked away in your freezer, saves the day and the lunch. Here it's fried chicken to eat with bread-and-butter sandwiches, then top off with popular brownies and mixed fruit salad. All will thaw by noontime. Separate containers keep the foods looking their best and are easy to stack and tote—even in a paper bag.

● ● ●

Plain-Good Beef Bounty
A perfect treat with yesterday's roast, and always a hit with men.
Makes 4 sandwiches

  4 tablespoons (½ stick) butter or margarine
  2 tablespoons bottled garlic spread
  8 large slices rye bread
 12 large thin slices roast beef
  ½ cup bottled Russian dressing
  4 small dill-pickle fans

1 Blend butter or margarine and garlic spread in a cup; spread on bread.
2 Fold roast-beef slices and arrange, overlapping, on 4 slices of bread; spoon Russian dressing over meat. Top each with a pickle fan; cover with remaining slices of bread.
3 Place each sandwich in a plastic bag, or wrap in wax paper, foil or transparent wrap.
Note—To make a pickle fan, cut pickle into 5 or 6 thin strips, cutting from tip end almost to stem; spread strips slightly to form a fan.

●

Chicken Jumbos
Sliced white meat teams with pineapple and a creamy dressing on raisin bread.
Makes 4 sandwiches

  1 can (about 1 pound, 5 ounces) pineapple spears
 16 thin slices cooked chicken breast
  8 slices unfrosted cinnamon-raisin bread, buttered
  ¼ cup mayonnaise or salad dressing
  2 tablespoons chopped pecans

1 Drain syrup from pineapple into a cup; set aside for Step 3.
2 Arrange chicken slices and pineapple spears, overlapping, on each of 4 slices of bread.
3 Blend mayonnaise or salad dressing, 1 tablespoon of the pineapple syrup and pecans in a cup; spoon a generous tablespoonful over filling for each sandwich. Cover with remaining slices of bread. (Chill remaining pineapple syrup to add to a breakfast beverage.)
4 Place each sandwich in a plastic bag, or wrap in wax paper, foil or transparent wrap.

●

Tuna Tugs
With carrots, onions, peanuts and tuna, they're a smorgasbord in a roll.
Makes 4 sandwiches

  4 hero rolls, split
  ½ cup mayonnaise or salad dressing

1289

1 teaspoon curry powder
1 cup grated carrots
⅓ cup chopped green onions
⅓ cup chopped peanuts
1 can (about 7 ounces) tuna, drained and flaked
1 tablespoon bottled oil-and-vinegar salad dressing

1 Hollow out bottom of each roll slightly with a fork. (Set pieces aside to make a crumb topping for a casserole.)
2 Mix mayonnaise or salad dressing and curry powder in a cup; spread on rolls. Spoon carrots, onions and peanuts, alternately, across bottom half of each roll.
3 Combine tuna and oil-and-vinegar dressing in a cup; toss lightly to mix; spoon in rows on top of vegetables. Cover with tops of rolls.
4 Place each sandwich in a plastic bag, or wrap in wax paper, foil or transparent wrap.

Sardine Line-ups
Tangy tomato dressing is the seasoner for tiny sardines and crackly cucumber.
Makes 4 sandwiches

8 slices white bread
Bottled tartare sauce
1 medium-size cucumber, scored and sliced thin
2 cans (about 4 ounces each) tiny sardines in oil, drained
¼ cup dairy sour cream
2 tablespoons catsup

1290

1 Spread bread with tartare sauce; layer part of the cucumber onto 4 slices. Arrange sardines in double rows on top; row remaining cucumber slices over sardines.
2 Blend sour cream and catsup in a cup; spoon a generous tablespoonful over filling for each sandwich. Cover with remaining slices of bread.
3 Place each sandwich in a plastic bag, or wrap in wax paper, foil or transparent wrap.

Cheese-Salad Rounds
Mellow cheese, crunchy nuts and apple and tangy grapes add up to a new flavor.
Makes 6 sandwiches

1 package (8 ounces) sliced process American cheese
1 cup halved seedless green grapes
½ cup chopped walnuts
¾ cup mayonnaise or salad dressing
⅛ teaspoon cardamom
12 slices round white bread
1 small red apple, halved, cored and sliced thin
Lemon juice

1 Dice cheese. (No need to separate slices.) Combine with grapes and walnuts in a small bowl. Blend ½ cup of the mayonnaise or salad dressing and cardamom in a cup; fold into cheese mixture. Spread remaining mayonnaise or salad dressing on bread.
2 Dip apple slices in lemon juice in a saucedish; arrange, skin side out, overlapping, around edges of 6 slices of bread; spread each with cheese mixture. Cover with remaining slices of bread.
3 Place each sandwich in a plastic bag, or wrap in wax paper, foil or transparent wrap.

Egg Whirligigs
Hard-cooked-egg slices top crisp onions for this sunny twist on a favorite.
Makes 4 sandwiches

4 split hamburger buns
Bottled sandwich spread
1 can (about 4 ounces) French fried onions
4 hard-cooked eggs, shelled and sliced lengthwise
6 stuffed green olives, sliced

1 Spread buns with sandwich spread; layer onions onto bottom halves.
2 Arrange egg slices, flower fashion, over onions; top with olive slices; garnish with parsley, if you wish. Cover with top halves of buns.
3 Place each sandwich in a plastic bag, or wrap in wax paper, foil or transparent wrap.

Asparagus-Egg Stacks
Be different and enjoy your egg as a savory custard sandwich filling.
Bake custard at 300° for 30 minutes. Makes 6 sandwiches

6 eggs, slightly beaten
2 cups milk

2 teaspoons salt
2 teaspoons dry mustard
⅛ teaspoon liquid red pepper seasoning
2 packages (10 ounces each) frozen asparagus spears, cooked, drained and chilled
12 slices firm-texture white bread, buttered
6 radishes, sliced thin

1 Beat eggs slightly with milk, salt, mustard and red pepper seasoning in a medium-size bowl. Strain into a lightly buttered baking pan, 9x9x2; cover. Set in a larger pan of boiling water.
2 Bake in slow oven (300°) 30 minutes, or until center is almost set but still soft. Remove at once from pan of water; chill.
3 Arrange 5 or 6 spears of asparagus on each of 6 slices of bread.
4 Cut chilled custard into six oblongs; place on asparagus; top with radish slices. Cover with remaining slices of bread.
5 Place each sandwich in a plastic bag, or wrap in wax paper, foil or transparent wrap.

Weight-Watchers' Mix-ups
Bless cottage cheese; it makes a protein-rich filling and saves calories.
Makes 6 sandwiches

1 can (8 ounces) diet-pack cling peach slices
1 carton (1 pound) cream-style cottage
cheese
¼ cup chopped parsley
12 slices whole-wheat bread
6 teaspoons bottled low-calorie whipped salad
dressing
6 maraschino cherries, halved

1 Drain syrup from peaches into a cup. Measure out 1 tablespoonful and blend into cottage cheese and parsley in a small bowl.
2 Spread bread with salad dressing, then spread each of 6 slices with about ⅓ cup cheese mixture. Top each with 2 peach slices and 2 cherry halves. Cover with remaining slices of bread.
3 Place each sandwich in a plastic bag, or wrap in wax paper, foil or transparent wrap.
Note—Count 213 calories for each sandwich.

●

Turkey Trio rolls main dish and salad into one wonderful lunch! Two of these hollowed-out dinner rolls hold a quick-fix meat filling; the other is heaped with peas and carrots in a

creamy dressing. Such embellishments as radish roses aren't really necessary, but they do add appetite appeal. Nice extra come-ons: Cranberry-orange relish to spoon from the jar, and a cupcake or wedge of pie for a finale.

Turkey Trios
Makes 6 servings, 3 sandwiches each

2 cans (5 ounces each) boned turkey,
chopped fine
3 wedges (1 ounce each) process Gruyère
cheese, diced fine
½ cup finely diced celery
1 tablespoon chopped parsley
½ teaspoon celery salt
½ cup mayonnaise or salad dressing
1 can (8 ounces) peas and carrots, drained
¼ teaspoon dillweed
18 small dinner rolls

1 Combine turkey, cheese, celery, parsley and celery salt in a medium-size bowl; fold in two thirds of the mayonnaise or salad dressing.
2 Fold remaining mayonnaise or salad dressing into peas and carrots and dillweed in a small bowl.
3 Cut a cone-shape piece from top of each roll. Spoon turkey salad into 12 of the rolls; spoon vegetable salad into remainder. Set cones back in place. Garnish each with a radish rose held in place with a wooden pick, if you wish. For each serving, wrap 2 turkey rolls and 1 vegetable roll together; pack with a small container of cranberry-orange relish.

Beefeater Rollup gets creative with what's left of yesterday's roast. To set it up for lunch, spread thin slices of meat with onion-seasoned cream cheese, then roll slices around carrot sticks and tuck into rye bread. For crunchy contrast, add layers of cucumber rounds. If your roast is all gone, buy enough slices to suffice at the delicatessen counter. Send-alongs: Cup of coleslaw, chocolate cake.

Beefeater Rollups
Makes 6 servings

1 package (8 ounces) cream cheese
1 envelope (2 packets) green-onion dip mix
2 teaspoons prepared horseradish

1291

Two very un-lunch-bag-like sandwiches: Turkey Trios—turkey salad tucked inside dinner rolls and Beefeater Rollups that team roast beef and an oniony spread.

1292

2 tablespoons milk
18 thin slices roast beef (about 2 pounds)
3 thin carrots, pared, quartered and cut in 3-inch lengths
12 large slices rye bread
4 tablespoons (½ stick) butter or margarine
Bibb lettuce
3 small cucumbers, sliced thin

1 Blend cream cheese, dip mix, horseradish and milk in a small bowl. Spread over roast-beef slices.
2 Place 1 or 2 carrot sticks at one end of each slice; roll up, jelly-roll fashion.
3 Spread bread with butter or margarine; layer each of 6 slices with lettuce, 3 roast-beef rolls and cucumber slices; top with remaining bread. Cut each sandwich in half; wrap.

●

Humpty-Dumpty might be called a Dagwood in disguise . . . a sandwich you build of layer upon layer of meats, cheese, lettuce, tomatoes, pickles—whatever your heart desires and refrigerator and kitchen cupboard have on hand!

Humpty-Dumpties
Makes 4 servings

8 slices home-style white bread

Two more luxurious lunch-bag sandwiches: Humpty-Dumpties, multi-layered with chicken and cheese and luscious lobster-salad Boothbay Rounders.

1 cup prepared sandwich spread
1 package (8 ounces) sliced process American cheese
   Romaine
3 medium-size tomatoes, sliced thin
1 package (4 ounces) sliced chicken white meat
1 jar (14 ounces) sliced sweet pickles, drained
1 package (5 ounces) sliced Canadian bacon
1 package (about 4 ounces) sliced tongue
   Cauliflowerets
   Green-pepper squares
   Cherry tomatoes

1 Spread bread with sandwich spread.

2 Layer each of 4 slices with cheese, romaine, tomato slices, chicken, pickles, Canadian bacon, cheese, tongue, romaine; top with remaining bread.
3 Cut each sandwich in half; wrap.
4 Thread 2 cauliflowerets, 2 green-pepper squares and a cherry tomato onto each of 4 skewers; wrap separately to pack with sandwiches.

Boothbay Rounder serves up a special for seafood fans: Hearty meal-on-a-hard-roll of lobster chunks with Russian-style dressing, Swiss cheese, lettuce and pickle. (Seaworthy substitutes: Tuna, crab, salmon.) Mound the halves separately for open-face eating, or "sandwich" them together. Round out the Rounder with hot beef broth in an individual vacuum bottle, easy-to-eat fresh fruit and cookies for dessert.

Boothbay Rounders
Makes 4 servings

2 cans (about 6 ounces each) lobster meat
½ cup mayonnaise or salad dressing
2 tablespoons catsup
2 tablespoons sweet-pickle relish
1 hard-cooked egg, shelled and diced
4 large hard rolls
  Boston lettuce
4 slices Swiss cheese (from an 8-ounce package)
4 medium-size sweet pickles

1 Drain the liquid from lobster; remove any bony tissue. Cut meat into bite-size pieces.
2 Mix mayonnaise or salad dressing, catsup and pickle relish in a small bowl; fold in egg.
3 Split rolls crosswise; spread with about half of the mayonnaise mixture.
4 Place lobster on bottom halves of rolls; top with remaining mayonnaise mixture. Place lettuce on top halves; fold cheese slices and place over lettuce; garnish each with a pickle fan. (To make, cut each pickle lengthwise into 5 or 6 thin slices; arrange slices to resemble a fan.)
5 Wrap sandwiches, open-face style, or put halves together first, then wrap.

Ham-Salad Triangles
Makes 6 servings

2 cups finely diced cooked ham
½ cup finely diced celery
1 teaspoon grated onion
⅓ cup mayonnaise or salad dressing
1 teaspoon prepared mustard
12 thin slices white bread, buttered

1 Mix ham, celery, onion, mayonnaise or salad dressing and mustard in a bowl.
2 Spread bread with ham-salad mixture to make 6 sandwiches.
3 Cut each sandwich diagonally into quarters; wrap.

1294

Country Burgers
Makes 8 servings

2 pounds ground beef
3 teaspoons seasoned salt
1 egg
½ cup dairy sour cream
1 teaspoon Worcestershire sauce
8 hamburger buns
½ cup prepared sandwich spread
1 can (3 ounces) French fried onions
  Romaine
4 medium-size tomatoes, sliced thin

1 Mix ground beef lightly with seasoned salt; shape into 8 thin 5-inch patties. Place on rack in broiler pan.
2 Broil, 6 inches from heat, 4 minutes; turn. Broil 2 minutes longer; remove from heat.
3 While patties cook, beat egg in a small bowl; stir in sour cream and Worcestershire sauce. Spoon 1 tablespoonful over each beef patty; return to broiler.
4 Broil 3 minutes, or just until topping is set; cool.
5 Spread buns with sandwich spread, then layer meat patties, onions, romaine and tomato slices into buns; wrap.

Shrimp Boats
Makes 4 servings

1 cup mayonnaise or salad dressing
¾ cup chopped celery
1 hard-cooked egg, shelled and chopped
1 tablespoon capers, drained
2 tablespoons chopped parsley
¼ teaspoon leaf tarragon, crumbled
4 club rolls
2 cans (5 ounces each) shrimps, drained and rinsed

1 Mix mayonnaise or salad dressing, celery, egg, capers, parsley and tarragon in a medium-size bowl.
2 Cut a thin slice from top of each roll; hollow out inside, leaving a ¼-inch-thick shell.
3 Spoon about half of the dressing into hollows

in rolls; top with shrimps, then remaining dressing. Cover with tops of rolls; wrap.

●

Vienna Salad Rolls
Makes 4 servings, 2 sandwiches each

2 cans (4 ounces each) Vienna sausages
¼ cup mayonnaise or salad dressing
2 tablespoons hamburger relish
¼ teaspoon liquid red pepper seasoning
1 cup finely shredded iceberg lettuce
1 jar (8 ounces) sliced pickled beets, well-drained
½ cup diced sweet onion
8 frankfurter rolls
4 tablespoons (½ stick) butter or margarine

1 Mash sausages with a fork in a medium-size bowl. (No need to drain first.) Stir in mayonnaise or salad dressing, hamburger relish, red pepper seasoning and lettuce.
2 Combine beets and onion in a small bowl.
3 Spread frankfurter rolls with butter or margarine. Spoon sausage mixture into 4 of the rolls and beet mixture into remainder. For each serving, wrap one sandwich of each kind together.

Dublin Dandies
Makes 6 servings

1 container (16 ounces) coleslaw
2 teaspoons caraway seeds
1 can (12 ounces) corned beef, chilled
2 small tomatoes
12 slices light pumpernickel
6 tablespoons (¾ stick) butter or margarine

1 Drain coleslaw well; mix with caraway seeds in a small bowl.
2 Cut corned beef into 12 slices; cut each tomato into 6 thin slices.
3 Spread pumpernickel with butter or margarine; layer each of 6 slices with corned beef, tomato slices and coleslaw, dividing·evenly; top with remaining bread.
4 Cut each sandwich in half diagonally; wrap.

●

Sardine Stacks
Makes 6 servings

1 cup mayonnaise or salad dressing
2 tablespoons lemon juice

2 tablespoons chili sauce
12 slices Vienna bread
6 hard-cooked eggs, shelled and sliced
3 cans (about 5 ounces each) sardines, drained
Iceberg lettuce

1 Blend mayonnaise or salad dressing, lemon juice and chili sauce in a small bowl; spread over bread.
2 Layer each of 6 slices with sliced eggs, sardines and lettuce; top with remaining bread. Cut each sandwich in half; wrap.

Braunschweiger Buildups
Makes 4 servings

1 piece braunschweiger, weighing ½ pound
2 tablespoons mayonnaise or salad dressing
½ teaspoon lemon juice
8 slices whole-wheat bread
3 tablespoons butter or margarine
2 medium-size tomatoes, sliced thin
¼ sweet Spanish onion, peeled and sliced thin

1 Peel casing from braunschweiger; mash meat with a fork in a medium-size bowl; blend in mayonnaise or salad dressing and lemon juice.
2 Spread bread with butter or margarine, then spread 4 of the slices with braunschweiger mixture. Cover with tomato and onion slices; top with remaining bread. Cut each sandwich in half; wrap.

Hot-Weather Westerns
Makes 6 servings

6 hard-cooked eggs, shelled
½ cup finely chopped green pepper
1 small onion, chopped fine (¼ cup)
¼ cup mayonnaise or salad dressing
1 teaspoon prepared mustard
½ teaspoon salt
Dash of pepper
12 slices white bread
6 tablespoons (¾ stick) butter or margarine
2 packages (6 ounces each) boiled ham

1 Mash eggs with a fork in a medium-size bowl;

fold in green pepper, onion, mayonnaise or salad dressing, mustard, salt and pepper.

2 Spread bread with butter or margarine; layer each of 6 slices with a slice of ham, egg salad and another slice of ham; top with remaining bread.

3 Cut each sandwich in half diagonally; wrap.

California Chicken Buns
Makes 6 servings

2 chicken breasts, weighing about 14 ounces each
2 cups water
1 medium-size onion, peeled and sliced
Few celery tops
1¼ teaspoons salt
3 peppercorns
1 can (about 14 ounces) pineapple tidbits, drained
1 cup diced celery
½ cup slivered almonds
½ cup mayonnaise or salad dressing
2 tablespoons milk
¼ teaspoons dry mustard
Dash of pepper
Lettuce
6 Vienna rolls, split and buttered
Cherry tomatoes

1 Combine chicken breasts, water, onion, celery tops, 1 teaspoon of the salt and peppercorns in a large saucepan; cover. Simmer 30 minutes, or until chicken is tender. Let stand until cool enough to handle, then skin chicken and take meat from bones; dice. (There should be about 2 cups.)

2 Combine chicken, pineapple, celery and almonds in a medium-size bowl. Blend mayonnaise or salad dressing, milk, remaining ¼ teaspoon salt, mustard and pepper in a small bowl; fold into chicken mixture.

3 Place lettuce on bottom halves of rolls; spoon salad mixture over lettuce; replace tops of rolls. Garnish each with a row of cherry tomatoes held in place with wooden picks; wrap.

1296

Turkey Clubs
Makes 4 servings

1 container (8 ounces) cream-style cottage cheese
1 can (8 ounces) apricot halves, drained and chopped
12 slices white sandwich bread
6 tablespoons mayonnaise or salad dressing
Iceberg lettuce
12 slices crisp bacon
2 packages (3 ounces each) sliced turkey breast

1 Blend cottage cheese and apricots in a small bowl.

2 Spread bread with mayonnaise or salad dressing; layer each of 4 slices with lettuce, cottage-cheese mixture, bacon, slice of bread, turkey, lettuce and remaining bread.

3 Cut each sandwich in half diagonally; wrap.

Bologna-Cheese Jumbos
Makes 4 servings

¼ cup mayonnaise or salad dressing
⅛ teaspoon dillweed
8 slices cracked-wheat bread
1 package (6 ounces) sliced bologna
1 package (8 ounces) sliced process American cheese
1 can (8 ounces) seasoned green beans, drained

1 Mix mayonnaise or salad dressing and dillweed in a small bowl; spread on bread.

2 Layer each of 4 slices with bologna, cheese, green beans, cheese and bologna; top with remaining bread. Cut each sandwich in half diagonally; wrap.

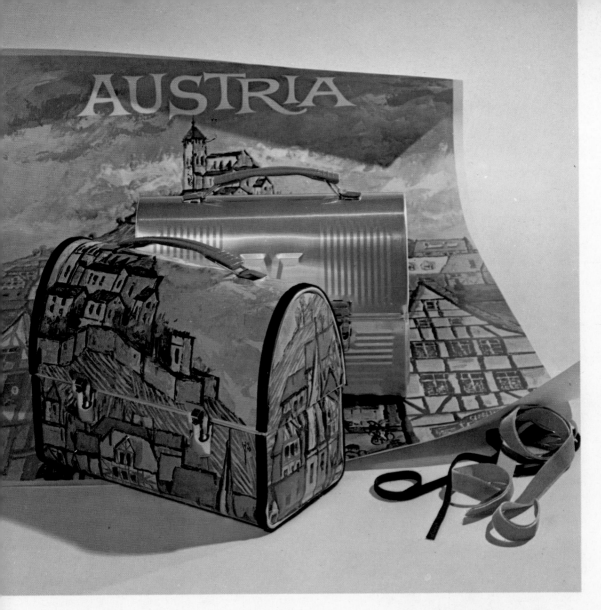

MAKE A CATCHY CARRYALL

Who says a lunch box has to look like a lunch box? Why not set (and steal) the scene with a one-of-a-kind lunch box that you've made yourself? It isn't difficult to do once you know how. Taking a cue from this one (first designed for exclusive boutiques by pacesetter Stella Jolles), find a travel poster you like (local travel agencies are good sources of them, often hand them out gratis), then cut out the parts you like and cover your lunch box, gluing the poster down with rubber cement. To make sure it really sticks, apply a thin coat to all surfaces of the lunch box, another thin coat to the cut-out poster. Wait for both to dry before sticking down the poster. It will stick fast—also in the minds of envious friends. You just could be a trend-setter. Another catchy carry-all, perfect for carrying a light lunch is a straw bag with a pop art placard.

LUNCHES AND BRUNCHES:
ALL-AMERICAN AND INTERNATIONAL BRUNCHES, LUNCHES FOR ALL SEASONS, A PICTURE PORTFOLIO OF PARTY TABLES, SHOWPIECE CENTERPIECES

Americans have always favored midday as a time to entertain—for lunches, for brunches, especially on weekends when friends and neighbors can be invited in about noon for food and drink. Lunches and brunches, somehow, seem more fun, more *flexible,* than dinners. Either one can be as big or little as the hostess wants, as informal or festive and, weather permitting, either can be served indoors or out.

No need for a special occasion although one *can* provide a theme, set the mood and get the party off to a flying start.

What to serve? No hard and fast rules although brunches often team the best of breakfast with the best of lunch or dinner—pancakes, for example, crowned not with syrup but with a savory meat or fish sauce. For big parties, it's best to serve buffet style from chafing dishes or warmers so that each guest can help himself. Needless to say, the dishes should be accommodating, preferably a stew or casserole with foods pre-cut in bite-size portions. Newburgs

are perfect and so are meat-ball recipes with plenty of gravy.

Sit-down lunches or brunches need not be any stiffer or more formal than the buffet style. A colorful, cleverly set table, a conversation-piece centerpiece will both help to make the mood spritely. In this section, you'll find a picture portfolio of lunch and brunch table settings, another of ingenious-but-easy-to-make centerpieces as well as a round-the-world, round-the-calendar collection of lunch and brunch menus for small casual gatherings and merry mob scenes.

1299

BRUNCHES: ALL-AMERICAN AND INTERNATIONAL

A CASUAL NEIGHBORHOOD BRUNCH FOR 4

Orange Juice
Ham-Pancake Shortcakes
Spiced Peaches
Basket Relishes
Milk　　　Coffee

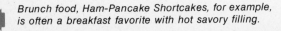

Brunch food, Ham-Pancake Shortcakes, for example, is often a breakfast favorite with hot savory filling.

A Sit-Down Sunday Brunch features puffy Gruyère Soufflé-Omelet, sizzling Sausage-Bacon Grill and rolls.

Ham-Pancake Shortcakes
Couldn't be easier! Pancakes and sauce both start with favorite mixes.
Makes 4 servings

> 1 can (12 ounces) pork luncheon meat
> 1 package (10 ounces) frozen cut green beans
> 1 small onion, chopped (¼ cup)
> ½ cup water
> 1 envelope (1½ ounces) à la king sauce mix
> 2 cups milk
> 12 large pancakes
> SPICED PEACHES (recipe follows)

1 Cut luncheon meat into ¼-inch-thick sticks about 2 inches long. Brown in a medium-size frying pan (no fat needed).
2 Add beans, onion and water; heat to boiling; cover. Simmer, stirring once, 15 minutes, or just until beans are crisply tender.
3 Prepare sauce mix with milk, following label directions, in top of double boiler over direct heat; stir in meat mixture. Keep hot over simmering water while making pancakes.
4 Make pancakes, using your favorite mix and following label directions. For each serving, put 3 together with sauce between. Top with a spiced peach half.

Spiced Peaches
Canned peach halves season in a honey-clove syrup to make this relishlike accompaniment.
Makes 4 servings

> 1 can (1 pound, 4 ounces) cling peach halves
> ¼ cup honey
> 6 whole cloves
> Cinnamon-sugar

1 Drain syrup from peaches into a small saucepan; place peaches in a medium-size bowl.
2 Stir honey and cloves into syrup; heat to boiling; simmer 15 minutes; strain over peaches. Chill—the longer, the better—to season and blend flavors.
3 When ready to serve, drain peaches; place in a shallow serving bowl; sprinkle with cinnamon-sugar.

A SIT-DOWN SUNDAY BRUNCH FOR 4

Chilled Fruit Juice
Gruyère Soufflé-Omelet
Sausage-Bacon Grill
Assorted Rolls
Strawberry Jam
Coffee   Milk

Gruyère Soufflé-Omelet

It puffs beautifully in an electric frying pan or in the oven. Do try it!
Makes 4 servings

    1 tablespoon grated onion
    6 tablespoons (¾ stick) butter or margarine
    6 tablespoons all-purpose flour
 1½ teaspoons salt
    ½ teaspoon curry powder
    ¼ teaspoon pepper
 1½ cups milk
    6 eggs, separated
    ½ cup grated Gruyère cheese

1 Sauté onion lightly in butter or margarine; stir in flour, salt, curry powder and pepper; cook, stirring constantly, just until bubbly. Stir in milk; continue cooking and stirring until sauce is very thick and boils 1 minute. Cool.
2 Beat egg whites until they form soft peaks; beat egg yolks well. Beat cooled sauce *very slowly* into egg yolks; fold in beaten whites.
3 Pour into a well-buttered 12-inch electric skillet or frying pan with ovenproof handle. Cook in electric skillet, following manufacturer's directions for omelet, 50 minutes. Sprinkle with cheese; cook 10 minutes longer. Or bake in frying pan in slow oven (325°) 30 minutes; add cheese; bake 5 minutes longer.

Sausage-Bacon Grill

These popular breakfast meats cook side by side in the oven with so little watching.
Bake at 325° for 40 minutes. Makes 4 servings

Place ½ pound sausage links on rack in broiler pan. Bake in slow oven (325°) 20 minutes; turn and push together. Place ½ pound bacon slices in a single layer alongside. Bake 20 minutes longer, or until done.

A SUMMER BUFFET BRUNCH FOR 6

Chilled Summer Bisque
Parsley-Butter Shrimps
Vegetable-Rice Salad
Hot Bread
Lemon Ice   Crisp Cookies
Iced Tea   Iced Coffee

Chilled Summer Bisque
Makes 6 servings

    1 envelope (2 in a package) smoky green-pea soup mix
    2 cups water
    1 tall can (14½ ounces) evaporated milk
    STICK CROUTONS (recipe follows)

1 Empty soup mix into a medium-size saucepan. Gradually stir in water until well blended. Heat, stirring constantly, just to boiling. Stir in evaporated milk; cover; simmer 15 minutes to blend flavors.
2 Pour into a pitcher; chill several hours or until icy cold. (For extra smoothness, beat soup at high speed in an electric blender container). Serve in bowls; sprinkle with STICK CROUTONS.
  STICK CROUTONS—Trim crusts from thin-sliced white bread. Cut bread into very thin matchlike sticks, then into 1-inch lengths. Arrange in single layer in shallow baking pan. Toast in slow oven (325°) 15 minutes, or until crisply golden.

Parsley-Butter Shrimps

Look for family-size bags of shrimps, ready to cook, in your supermarket's freezer cabinet.
Makes 6 servings

    4 tablespoons (½ stick) butter or margarine
    1 bag (1½ pounds) frozen deveined, shelled, raw shrimps ·
    2 tablespoons lemon juice
    2 tablespoons chopped parsley

1 Melt butter or margarine in large frying pan; add frozen shrimps. (No need to thaw.)
2 Simmer slowly, stirring often, 20 to 25 minutes, or until shrimps are tender.
3 Sprinkle lemon juice and parsley over; toss lightly to mix.

1301

Vegetable-Rice Salad
Makes 6 servings

    1 cup uncooked regular rice
    1 envelope Parmesan salad-dressing mix
    Salad oil
    Cider vinegar

ALL-AMERICAN AND INTERNATIONAL

2 cans (1 pound each) green beans
1 large tomato, cut in 6 wedges
1 hard-cooked egg, shelled and sieved
  Paprika

1 Cook rice, following label directions.
2 While rice cooks, make Parmesan salad dressing with salad oil and vinegar, following label directions. Heat beans in medium-size saucepan; drain.
3 Combine warm rice, beans and ½ cup salad dressing in large bowl; toss lightly to mix.
4 Spoon into a serving bowl; top with a ring of tomato wedges. Spoon sieved hard-cooked egg into center; sprinkle with paprika. Spoon PARSLEY-BUTTER SHRIMPS into a bowl on serving tray; spoon salad around bowl, arranging garnish in a semicircle.

BEFORE-THE-GAME BRUNCH FOR 6

Mexican Mocha
Cucumber Rolls
Egg Squares
Corned-Beef Triangles
Little Fruit-and-Cheese Tray

Mexican Mocha
Makes 6 servings, about 1¼ cups each

¾ cup instant cocoa mix
⅓ cup freeze-dried instant coffee
3 cups water
2 cups milk
1 cup light cream or table cream
1 teaspoon orange extract

1 Blend cocoa mix, coffee, water and milk in a large saucepan. Heat, stirring often, to boiling; remove from heat.
2 Stir in ½ cup of the cream; pour into heated mugs.
3 Stir orange extract into remaining ½ cup cream; float a thin layer on top of each serving.

1303

Cucumber Rolls
Makes 24 small sandwiches

12 slices soft white bread
⅓ cup butter or margarine, softened
⅓ cup mayonnaise or salad dressing
3 tablespoons chopped parsley

A creamy-cool pea bisque, Parsley-Butter Shrimps and Vegetable-Rice Salad add up to Summer Buffet Brunch.

1 medium-size cucumber, pared, seeded, and
   cut in 24 thin strips
   Salt
   Paprika
   Watercress

1 Trim crusts from bread; roll each slice thin
with a rolling pin.
2 Blend butter or margarine, mayonnaise or
salad dressing and parsley in a small bowl;
spread on bread.
3 Sprinkle cucumber strips lightly with salt and
paprika; place 2 strips on one end of each bread
slice; roll up tightly, jelly-roll fashion. Wrap and
chill.
4 When ready to serve, cut each roll in half;
tuck a tiny sprig of watercress in end of each
half.

Egg Squares
Makes 24 small sandwiches

12 slices whole-wheat bread
   Butter or margarine, softened
 3 hard-cooked eggs, shelled and mashed
¼ cup mayonnaise or salad dressing
 2 teaspoons freeze-dried chives
 2 teaspoons horseradish-mustard
¼ teaspoon salt

1 Spread each slice of bread with butter or
margarine.
2 Mix eggs, mayonnaise or salad dressing,
chives, horseradish-mustard and salt in a small
bowl; spread over half of the bread slices. Top
with remaining slices, sandwich style. Wrap and
chill.
3 When ready to serve, cut each sandwich in
quarters.

1304

●

Corned-Beef Triangles
Makes 24 small sandwiches

24 slices party-size rye bread
   Butter or margarine, softened
 1 can (4½ ounces) corned-beef spread
 2 tablespoons chopped drained watermelon
   pickle or preserves
 2 tablespoons dairy sour cream

1 Spread each slice of bread with butter or
margarine.

2 Mix corned-beef spread, watermelon pickle
and sour cream in a small bowl; spread over
half of the bread. Top with remaining slices,
sandwich style. Wrap and chill.
3 When ready to serve, halve each sandwich
diagonally.

A LIGHT LADIES' BRUNCh FOR 8

Seafood-Stuffed Crêpes
Buttered Asparagus
Bouquet Salads
Raspberry Sherbet
Chocolate Cookies
Iced Tea

Seafood-Stuffed Crêpes
Thin-thin pancakes rolled around a crunchy
salmon-tuna filling bake in a creamy sauce.
Bake at 350° for 30 minutes. Makes 8 servings

Filling and Sauce
1 can (about 8 ounces) salmon, drained,
  boned, and flaked
1 can (about 7 ounces) tuna, drained and
  flaked
1 can (5 ounces) water chestnuts, drained and
  chopped
  OR: ½ cup finely diced celery
1 tablespoon minced onion
5 tablespoons butter or margarine
⅓ cup sifted all-purpose flour
1 teaspoon salt
⅛ teaspoon pepper
2 cups milk
4 tablespoons grated Parmesan cheese
1 tablespoon lemon juice
Crêpes
¾ cup sifted all-purpose flour
1 tablespoon sugar
½ teaspoon salt
3 eggs
1 cup milk
1 tablespoon melted butter or margarine
Topping
¼ cup cream for whipping

1 Make filling and sauce: Mix salmon, tuna and
water chestnuts or celery in a medium-size
bowl.
2 Sauté onion in butter or margarine just until
soft in a medium-size saucepan. Blend in flour,
salt and pepper; cook, stirring all the time, just

Ideal for a ladies' brunch: Seafood-Stuffed Crêpes.

until mixture bubbles. Stir in milk; continue cooking and stirring until sauce thickens and boils 1 minute. Remove from heat; blend in 2 tablespoons of the cheese and lemon juice. (Save remaining cheese for Step 8.)

3 Stir 1 cup sauce into tuna-salmon mixture; set remaining aside for Step 8.

4 Make crêpes: Measure flour, sugar and salt into sifter. Beat eggs until thick in a medium-size bowl; sift dry ingredients over; beat just until smooth. Stir in milk and butter or margarine.

5 Heat an 8-inch heavy frying pan slowly; test temperature by sprinkling in a few drops of water. When drops bounce about, temperature is right. Grease pan with butter or margarine.

6 Pour batter, a scant ⅓ cup at a time, into pan, tilting pan to cover bottom completely. Bake 1 to 2 minutes, or until top is set and underside golden; turn; brown other side. Repeat with remaining batter, lightly buttering pan before each baking, to make 8 crêpes.

7 Spoon about ⅓ cup filling into center of each crêpe as it's baked; roll up and place, seam side down, in a shallow baking dish.

8 Make topping: Beat cream until stiff in a small bowl; fold into remaining sauce from Step 3; spoon over crêpes. Sprinkle with saved 2 tablespoons Parmesan cheese.

9 Bake in moderate oven (350°) 30 minutes, or until filling is hot and cheese is golden. Garnish with parsley, if you wish.

Bouquet Salads
Simple to make, and a dash of Worcestershire sauce gives the dressing extra zip.
Makes 8 servings

1 large head Boston lettuce
6 tablespoons vegetable oil
2 tablespoons cider vinegar
½ teaspoon sugar
¼ teaspoon salt
½ teaspoon Worcestershire sauce
½ bunch watercress

1 Tear lettuce into bite-size pieces in 8 individual salad bowls or a large bowl.

2 Combine vegetable oil, vinegar, sugar, salt and Worcestershire sauce in a jar with tight-fitting lid; shake well to mix. Drizzle over salads; garnish with watercress.

A GALA CHRISTMAS BRUNCH FOR 8

Traditional Holiday Eggnog
Creamed Chicken Veronique
on toasted Muffins or Biscuits
Cranberry Jelly   Spiced Cantaloupe Pickle
Christmas-Tree Cheese Mold
Baby Gouda Bowl
Finger Fruits
Coffee

Traditional Holiday Eggnog
Makes 8 to 10 punch-cup servings

9 eggs
1 cup very fine granulated sugar
2 cups bourbon
½ cup cognac
1 teaspoon vanilla
2 cups light cream or table cream
3 cups heavy cream
  Grated nutmeg

1 Separate eggs, placing yolks in a large bowl and whites in a second large bowl.

2 Add sugar to egg yolks; beat until fluffy-thick. Stir in bourbon, cognac, vanilla and light cream. Chill several hours, or until very cold.

3 Beat egg whites until they stand in firm peaks. Beat heavy cream until stiff in a large bowl. Fold beaten egg whites, then whipped cream into egg-yolk mixture; pour into a large punch bowl. Sprinkle with grated nutmeg. Ladle into punch cups.

Creamed Chicken Veronique
This popular dish goes gourmet-fancy with halved green grapes and toasty slivered almonds.
Makes 8 servings

3 chicken breasts (about 12 ounces each)
1 small onion, quartered
  Few celery tops
2 teaspoons salt
6 peppercorns
1 cup water
½ cup (1 stick) butter or margarine
½ cup sifted all-purpose flour
⅛ teaspoon pepper
  Dash of nutmeg
1½ cups table cream or light cream
1½ cups milk
1 cup halved seeded grapes
½ cup toasted slivered almonds (from an about-5-ounce can)
  Parsley

1 Simmer chicken with onion, celery tops, 1

Christmas is cup-of-cheer time so what better than a whole brunch built around Traditional Holiday Eggnog?

The best holiday insurance against drop-in guests are nibbles galore. These are unique—mountains of berries and melon balls and a bowl of snowy sour cream for "dunking." There are rolls, too, jams and tea.

teaspoon salt, peppercorns and water in a large saucepan 30 minutes, or until tender. Remove chicken from broth; cool until easy to handle. Strain broth into a 2-cup measure; add water, if needed, to make 1½ cups.

2 Remove skin and bones from chicken; dice meat. There should be 4 cups. (Broth and chicken can be fixed the day before, then covered and chilled until you're ready to make sauce and finish dish.)

3 Melt butter or margarine in a large saucepan.

Blend in flour, remaining 1 teaspoon salt, pepper and nutmeg; cook, stirring all the time, just until mixture bubbles. Stir in the 1½ cups chicken broth, cream and milk slowly; continue cooking and stirring until sauce thickens and boils 1 minute.

4 Stir in diced chicken; heat until bubbly, then fold in grapes and almonds. Spoon into a chafing dish or heated serving bowl; garnish with a wreath of parsley. Serve on toasted hot muffins or biscuits.

Christmas-Tree Cheese Mold
Swags of chopped parsley trim this tree-shape mold of simply seasoned cream cheese.
Makes 8 servings

1 package (8 ounces) cream cheese, softened
½ cup crumbled blue cheese (about 2 ounces)
⅛ teaspoon curry powder
¼ cup finely chopped parsley
    Pimiento

1 Blend cream cheese, blue cheese and curry powder in a small bowl; chill until firm enough to handle.
2 Turn out onto a sheet of wax paper or foil; mold into a cone about 5 inches high.
3 Press an inch-wide strip of wax paper or foil daigonally around cheese "tree" to resemble swags, pleating paper, if needed, to shape to cheese. Roll "tree" in chopped parsley; chill again until firm.
4 When ready to serve, gently peel off strips of paper. Decorate top with a tiny pimiento star.

A FESTIVE NEW YEAR'S BRUNCH FOR 24

Champagne Punch
Beef and Apple Balls   Savory Almond Sauce
Buttered Noodles   Fluffy Boiled Rice
Seafood Salad Soufflé
Party Appetizer Vegetables
Mini-Parker House Rolls
Rainbow Cream Ring Strawberry Sundae
Sauce
White Holiday Fruit Cake
Coffee

Champagne Punch
Makes about 24 punch-cup servings

½ cup light corn syrup
½ cup brandy
1 bottle (4/5 quart) Chablis, chilled
1 bottle (28 ounces) carbonated water, chilled
1 bottle (4/5 quart) champagne, chilled
    Ice cubes
    Peel from 1 lemon, cut in continuous strip

1 Mix corn syrup and brandy in punch bowl until well blended; stir in Chablis.
2 Just before serving, add carbonated water and champagne. Carefully add ice cubes and lemon peel.

Beef and Apple Balls
Bake at 400° for 10 minutes. Makes 24 servings

4½ pounds ground lean beef

3 large green apples, pared, quartered and cored
3 large pears, pared, quartered and cored
3 small Bermuda onions, peeled and quartered
3 small green peppers, halved and seeded
5 eggs
3 cups crushed corn flakes
1 tablespoon salt
½ teaspoon pepper
2 teaspoons ground nutmeg
¼ teaspoon garlic powder
⅛ teaspoon ground allspice
    SAVORY ALMOND SAUCE (recipe follows)

1 Put beef, apples, pears, onions and green peppers through food chopper, using finest blade; mix in a very large bowl or kettle with eggs, corn flakes and seasonings.
2 Shape lightly into marble-size balls (recipe makes about 300); place in single layers in buttered shallow baking pans (you'll need about 3 pans or, at least, to bake the balls in 3 batches). Bake in a hot oven (400°) 10 minutes; then broil for a minute or two to brown tops.
3 When ready to serve, heat meat balls in SA-

1309

One of the best merry-makers: Champagne Punch.

VORY ALMOND SAUCE until heated through; spoon into large tureen and serve with buttered noodles and/or fluffy cooked rice.

●

Savory Almond Sauce
Makes about 2 quarts

6 tablespoons butter or margarine
1½ cups canned slivered blanched almonds
6 tablespoons cornstarch
3 tablespoons brown sugar
4½ cups water
6 chicken-bouillon cubes
3 jars (baby-pack) strained apricots and apples
3 cups halved seedless green grapes

1 Melt butter or margarine in a large saucepan; add almonds and cook over low heat, stirring often, until golden-brown. Remove from heat.
2 Blend cornstarch, brown sugar and water into almonds. Add bouillon cubes and cook over low heat, stirring constantly, until bouillon cubes are dissolved and sauce is thick and clear.
3 Stir in strained apricots and apples, also the grapes. Heat to boiling before adding meat balls.

Seafood Salad Soufflé
No need to serve extra dressing with this beauty, as it's molded into both layers.
Makes 24 servings

Lime Layer
1 package (3 ounces) lime-flavor gelatin
1 cup boiling water
1 cup (8-ounce carton) dairy sour cream
½ cup mayonnaise or salad dressing
2 tablespoons lemon juice
½ teaspoon salt
Few drops liquid red pepper seasoning
1 large cucumber

1310

Seafood Layer
2 envelopes unflavored gelatin
1½ cups water
2 cans (1 pound each) salmon
1 can (about 7 ounces) crabmeat
½ cup mayonnaise or salad dressing
2 tablespoons lemon juice
1 teaspoon salt
¼ teaspoon freshly ground pepper
2 egg whites
1 cup cream for whipping
Red food coloring

1 Make lime layer: Dissolve lime gelatin in boiling water in a medium-size bowl; stir in sour cream, mayonnaise or salad dressing, lemon juice, salt and red pepper seasoning. Chill 30 minutes, or until as thick as unbeaten egg white.
2 Cut about 12 thin even slices from cucumber, then trim a sliver from each so it will stand flat around edge of mold; set aside for Step 8. Pare remaining cucumber and trimmings and chop fine; fold into thickened lime-gelatin mixture; pour into a 12-cup fancy tube mold. Chill 30 minutes, or just until sticky-firm.
3 While mixture in mold chills, make seafood layer: Soften gelatin in ½ cup of the water in a small saucepan; heat, stirring constantly, until gelatin dissolves; remove from heat. Stir in remaining 1 cup water.
4 Drain both cans of salmon; bone and flake into a medium-size bowl. Drain crabmeat; flake and remove bony tissue, if any; add to salmon.
5 Combine ⅓ each of the seafood and gelatin mixtures at a time in an electric-blender container; cover. Beat at high speed until smooth; pour into a large bowl. Stir in mayonnaise or salad dressing, lemon juice, salt and pepper.
6 Beat egg whites until they stand in firm peaks in a small bowl. Beat cream until stiff in a medium-size bowl. Fold beaten egg whites, then whipped cream into seafood mixture. Tint salmon color with a few drops food coloring. Carefully spoon over sticky-firm layer in mold. Chill several hours, or until firm. (Overnight is best.)
7 When ready to serve, run a sharp-tip, thin-blade knife around top of salad, then dip mold *very quickly* in and out of a pan of hot water. Cover mold with a serving plate; turn upside down; gently lift off mold.
8 Stand saved cucumber slices, flat edge down, around side of salad. Fill center with a few crisp romaine or curly endive leaves, if you wish.

Party Appetizer Vegetables
Tart lemon butter turns crisply cooked vegetables into a delightfully different titbit.
Makes 24 servings

1 bunch broccoli (about 2 pounds)
1 medium-size cauliflower
2 packages (9 ounces each) frozen artichoke hearts
2 tablespoons finely chopped onion

½ cup (1 stick) butter or margarine
¼ teaspoon salt
¼ teaspoon paprika
3 tablespoons lemon juice
 Diced pimiento

1 Cut broccoli flowerets from stems, saving stems to cook for another meal; halve large flowerets. Trim green leafy stems from cauliflower; break cauliflower into flowerets; halve any large ones.
2 Cook both vegetables, covered, in boiling salted water in separate large saucepans 8 minutes, or just until crisply tender; drain. Cook artichoke hearts, following label directions; drain. Keep all hot.
3 Sauté onion in butter or margarine in a small frying pan 2 minutes; remove from heat. Stir in salt, paprika and lemon juice.
4 When ready to serve, arrange artichoke hearts at either end of a large chafing dish or keep-hot server; arrange broccoli and cauliflowerets in center. Drizzle lemon butter over all. Sprinkle artichoke hearts with pimiento.

Mini-Parker House Rolls
Each of these buttery gems is just the right size to make into a two-bite sandwich.
Bake at 450° for 15 minutes. Makes 80 tiny rolls

½ cup (1 stick) butter or margarine
 4 packages refrigerated plain or buttermilk
 biscuits

1 Melt butter or margarine in a jelly-roll pan, 15x10x1, while oven heats.
2 Separate the 10 biscuits in each package; cut each in half. (Scissors make the job go fast.) Roll each half into a tiny ball, then flatten with a glass to a 2-inch round; fold round in half.
3 Roll in melted butter or margarine in pan to coat all over, then arrange in a single layer in same pan. (So rolls keep a trim neat shape, arrange in 10 rows of eight each.)
4 Bake in very hot oven (450°) 15 minutes, or until golden. Serve hot.
Hostess Note—Rolls may be baked ahead, if you wish, then reheated just before serving time.

Rainbow Cream Ring
Simple molding trick turns store-bought ice cream into this sweet splurge.
Makes 12 servings

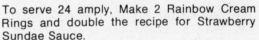
Easy to make and always a hit: Rainbow Cream Ring.

2 pints vanilla ice cream, slightly softened
2 pints raspberry sherbet, slightly softened
 STRAWBERRY SUNDAE SAUCE (recipe follows)

1 Spoon part of the vanilla ice cream and raspberry sherbet, alternately, into an 8-cup ring mold to make a layer of eight sections. Repeat with remaining ice cream and sherbet until all are used. Cover mold.
2 Freeze several hours, or until very firm.
3 When ready to serve, loosen mold around top with a knife, then dip mold *very quickly* in and out of a pan of warm water; invert onto a serving plate. Carefully lift off mold. (Work quickly so ice cream doesn't melt.)
4 Cut into wedges with a sharp knife; place on serving plates; serve with STRAWBERRY SUNDAE SAUCE.

To serve 24 amply, Make 2 Rainbow Cream Rings and double the recipe for Strawberry Sundae Sauce.

Strawberry Sundae Sauce
Keep a jar of this fresh-flavor fruit topping on hand for spur-of-the-moment entertaining.
Makes 3 cups

 3 packages (10 ounces each) frozen sliced
 strawberries, partly thawed
 1 cup sugar
¼ cup water

1 Combine 1 package of the sliced strawberries and syrup, sugar and water in a medium-size saucepan. (Set remaining strawberries aside for Step 3.)
2 Heat slowly, stirring constantly, to boiling,

1311

then cook, stirring several times, 10 minutes, or until slightly thickened.

3 Pour over remaining strawberries in a medium-size bowl; stir lightly until strawberries are completely thawed. Store in a covered jar in the refrigerator.

To be certain of having enough for a big party, Make 2 Fruit Cakes.

White Christmas Fruit Cake
Tender white cake all aglitter with rainbow fruits. Add its tangy glaze on serving day.
Bake at 275° for 3 hours. Makes one 8-inch round cake

  3 cups (3 eight-ounce jars) chopped mixed
    candied fruits
2⅔ cups (2 cans, about 3 ounces each) flaked
    coconut
1½ cups golden raisins
1½ cups coarsely chopped blanched almonds
1½ teaspoons grated orange peel
3¾ cups sifted cake flour
1½ teaspoons baking powder
  ¾ teaspoon salt
  ¾ cup (1½ sticks) butter or margarine
1½ cups sugar
  6 eggs
  ½ cup apple juice
  ⅓ cup orange juice
    ORANGE BUTTER (recipe follows)

1 Grease bottom and side of an 8-inch tube pan; line bottom with wax paper; grease paper.
2 Combine candied fruits, coconut, raisins, almonds and orange peel in large bowl.
3 Sift flour, baking powder and salt over fruit; mix well.
4 Cream butter or margarine with sugar until fluffy in medium-size bowl; beat in eggs, one at a time; stir in apple and orange juices. Pour over fruit mixture; fold and blend until mixed thoroughly. Spoon batter into prepared pan, pressing down firmly with a spoon to make top even.
5 Bake in very slow oven (275°) 3 hours, or until firm on top.
6 Cool cake completely in pan. Loosen around edge with knife; turn out on wire rack; remove paper. Wrap in wax paper, foil or transparent wrap until ready to use. (This cake freezes perfectly. Or it will keep fresh and moist for 2 to

1312

3 weeks if stored in a tightly fastened plastic bag.)
7 On serving day, frost top with ORANGE BUTTER ICING, letting frosting drip down over side and center tube. Decorate with whole candied red cherries and pecan halves, if you wish.

  ORANGE BUTTER ICING—Combine 1 tablespoon melted butter or margarine, 1 tablespoon orange juice and 1½ cups sifted 10X (confectioners' powdered) sugar in 2-cup measure; beat until smooth and creamy. Makes about ¾ cup.

TWO BRUNCHES WITH AN INTERNATIONAL FLAVOR

AN ITALIAN FESTA FOR 8

Souffléed Seafood Ramekins   Baked Clams
Veal Roast Italiano with Tuna Sauce
Fettuccine
Salad Bar with Minted Orange Sections,
Relish Mushrooms,   Eggplant Napoli
Garlic Loaf
Fruit-and-Cheese Buffet

Souffléed Seafood Ramekins
Puffy golden caps crown little shells filled with crab and shrimps in creamy sauce.
Bake at 375° for 30 minutes. Makes 8 servings

  1 can (5 ounces) deveined shrimps
  1 can (about 7 ounces) crabmeat
  1 teaspoon grated onion
  3 tablespoons butter or margarine
  3 tablespoons all-purpose flour
  ⅛ teaspoon salt
    Dash of ground nutmeg
1½ cups milk
  1 egg, separated
  ½ teaspoon lemon juice
  ½ cup mayonnaise or salad dressing

1 Drain shrimps, then rinse. Drain crabmeat and flake, removing bony tissue, if any. Set both aside for Step 4.
2 Sauté onion lightly in butter or margarine in a medium-size saucepan; stir in flour, salt and nutmeg, then milk. Cook, stirring constantly, until sauce thickens and boils 1 minute.
3 Beat egg yolk slightly in a small bowl. (Set white aside for Step 6.) Blend ½ cup of the hot sauce into egg yolk, then stir back into remaining in saucepan. Heat, stirring constantly, 1 minute longer; remove from heat.

4 Stir in shrimps, crabmeat and lemon juice. Spoon into 8 small scallop shells or broilerproof serving dishes; place on a cookie sheet for easy handling. Chill if made ahead.

5 Just before serving, bake in moderate oven (375°) 30 minutes, or until bubbly hot; remove from oven for next step. Set temperature control to broil.

6 Beat saved egg white until it stands in firm peaks in a small bowl; fold in mayonnaise or salad dressing. Spoon on top of hot seafood mixture, dividing evenly.

7 Broil 2 to 3 minutes, or until topping is puffed and golden-brown. Arrange on a large platter; garnish with lemon wedges dipped in paprika, if you wish.

Note—To keep seafood hot for serving outdoors, heat about 2 pounds rock salt in a shallow metal pan in oven while baking ramekins. Remove salt from oven; arrange hot seafood shells on top.

Baked Clams

Each little shell holds a savory stuffing of clams, cheese and parsley.
Bake at 375° for 15 minutes. Makes 8 servings

> 1 can (about 8 ounces) minced clams, drained
> 1½ cups soft bread crumbs (3 slices)
> ¼ cup grated Cheddar cheese
> 1 tablespoon chopped parsley
> ¼ teaspoon garlic salt
> 2 tablespoons olive oil or vegetable oil
> ½ teaspoon lemon juice

1 Combine all ingredients in a small bowl; toss lightly to mix; spoon into 8 scrubbed clam shells or small foil muffin-pan cups. Place shells or cups on a cookie sheet for easy handling. Chill if made ahead.

2 Just before serving, bake in moderate oven (375°.) 15 minutes, or until golden. Arrange on platter with SOUFFLÉED SEAFOOD RAMEKINS (*recipe precedes*).

Veal Roast Italiano

When sliced, meat is dotted with rounds of spicy-hot pepperoni.
Roast at 325° about 2½ to 3 hours. Makes 8 to 12 servings

4 to 5 pounds leg of veal roast

> *OR: 4 to 5 pounds rump of veal*
> 1 package (about 8 ounces) pepperoni
> 2 teaspoons seasoned salt
> 1 sweet green pepper, seeded and cut into squares
> 1 sweet red pepper, seeded and cut into squares
> Bottled Italian-style salad dressing
> TUNA SAUCE (recipe follows)

1 Bone leg or rump roast, or ask your meatman to do it for you. Tie meat with string to hold in shape.

2 Cut pepperoni into 4 or 5 pieces; insert one piece into each hole where bone was removed. Cut several more holes straight through roast, then fill with the remaining pieces of pepperoni.

3 Rub meat all over with seasoned salt. Place on a rack in roasting pan but do not add any water or cover pan. If using a meat thermometer, insert bulb into center of meat.

4 Roast in slow oven (325°), allowing 35 minutes per pound or 2½ to 3 hours, or until thermometer registers 170°. Remove from oven; cool, then chill until serving time.

5 Pour boiling water over green and red pepper squares in a bowl; let stand 5 minutes; drain, then drizzle lightly with salad dressing.

6 When ready to serve, carve part of roast, then place slices and remaining roast on a large platter; garnish with seasoned pepper squares. Serve with TUNA SAUCE.

Tuna Sauce

This creamy topper, sparked with anchovies and capers may surprise you, but it contrasts delightfully with veal.
Makes about 1½ cups

> 1 can (about 7 ounces) tuna
> ½ cup chicken broth (from a 14-ounce can)
> ¼ cup cream for whipping
> 2 drops liquid red pepper seasoning
> 2 anchovy fillets (from a 2-ounce can), chopped
> 2 tablespoons capers, well drained
> 1 tablespoon chopped pimiento

1 Combine tuna and chicken broth in an electric-blender container; cover. Beat several minutes, or until thick and smooth.

2 Add cream and liquid red pepper seasoning;

1313

beat about a minute longer; stir in anchovies, capers and pimiento.

3 Pour into a serving bowl. (Make this sauce no longer than an hour ahead and keep it chilled, as it tends to separate.)

Fettuccine

The popular Italian favorite: Noodles tossed with lots of butter, cream, and grated Parmesan cheese.
Makes 8 servings

2 packages (8 ounces each) regular noodles
½ cup (1 stick) butter or margarine
1 cup cream for whipping
1 cup grated Parmesan cheese

1 Cook noodles in a kettle, following label directions; drain; return to kettle.

2 Heat butter or margarine with cream just until butter melts in a small saucepan; pour over noodles; sprinkle with cheese. Toss well, reaching into bottom of kettle each time, until noodles are evenly coated.

3 Spoon into a chafing dish or keep-hot server; serve with freshly ground pepper to sprinkle over, if you wish.

Salad Bar

Everyone chooses his favorite toppings to toss with his own salad.
Makes 8 servings

8 cups broken mixed salad greens
   Bottled Italian-style salad dressing
   MINTED ORANGE SECTIONS *(recipe follows)*
   RELISH MUSHROOMS *(recipe follows)*
   EGGPLANT NAPOLI *(recipe follows)*

1 Place greens in a large glass salad bowl; toss with just enough salad dressing to coat lightly. Garnish top with a radish rose, if you wish, then set bowl in center of a large tray.

2 Surround with small bowls of MINTED ORANGE SECTIONS, RELISH MUSHROOMS, and EGGPLANT NAPOLI.

1314

Minted Orange Sections

They taste invitingly cool—and make such a colorful touch on a salad tray.
Makes 1¼ cups

3 large seedless oranges
2 tablespoons lemon juice
3 teaspoons honey
1 teaspoon chopped fresh mint

1 Peel oranges, then section fruit into a small bowl.

2 Combine lemon juice, honey and mint in a cup; pour over orange sections; toss lightly to mix. Chill several hours to season.

3 Arrange in a small serving bowl; garnish with mint leaves, if you wish.

Relish Mushrooms

These zippy titbits owe their distinctive flavor to a simple tarragon dressing.
Makes about 1 cup

¼ cup white vinegar
2 tablespoons sugar
¼ teaspoon leaf tarragon, crushed
2 cans (3 or 4 ounces each) whole
   mushrooms, drained

1 Combine vinegar, sugar and tarragon in a small bowl; stir until sugar dissolves.

2 Drain mushrooms, saving liquid to add to soup or gravy; stir mushrooms into vinegar mixture. Chill several hours to season.

3 Spoon into a small serving bowl; garnish with onion rings and a sprig of fresh tarragon, if you wish.

Eggplant Napoli

Small cubes of eggplant are sautéed first, then seasoned, salad style. Any leftover keeps perfectly in the refrigerator.
Makes about 3 cups

1 small eggplant (about 1 pound)

½ cup olive oil or vegetable oil
½ cup cider vinegar
1 tablespoon sugar
½ teaspoon salt
¼ teaspoon onion salt
¼ teaspoon leaf oregano, crumbled
⅛ teaspoon celery seeds
    Dash of garlic powder

1 Cut eggplant in ½-inch cubes but do not pare.
2 Sauté, stirring several times, in olive oil or vegetable oil in a medium-size frying pan 5 minutes, or until soft and lightly browned. Spoon into a medium-size bowl.
3 Mix remaining ingredients in a 1-cup measure; pour over eggplant; toss lightly to mix. Chill several hours to season.
4 Spoon part into a small serving bowl; garnish with an onion ring and cherry-tomato halves sprinkled with chopped parsley, if you wish.

Fruit-and-Cheese Buffet
This colorful arrangement can be your centerpiece as well as dessert.

Use a decorative tiered server or stand three compotes of graduating sizes on top of one another to make a tall server. Fill tiers with favorite summer fruits, a selection of dessert cheeses and crown all with a ruffly cantaloupe basket heaped with rosy-red watermelon balls. For fruits, use whole plums, peaches, bunches of green and purple grapes, and papaya quarters. For cheeses, we show Bel Paese, Camembert, Roquefort, provolone, and grappe (a strong-flavor, oyster-white cheese covered with tiny grape seeds). To make the cantaloupe basket, halve a large cantaloupe crosswise, scoop out seeds, pare, and scallop top edge. Cut balls from ripe watermelon and heap into cantaloupe.

● ● ●

A DANISH SMØRREBRØD FOR 8

Danish Appetizer Meat Balls
Golden Finger Rolls
Smørrebrød Tray
Party Cheese Platter
Kraemmerhuse
(Cream Horns)
with Fresh Strawberries
Coffee

SMØRREBRØD TRAY

In Denmark, *smørrebrød* means "spread bread" and may refer either to big open-face wholemeal sandwiches or a variety of dainty appetizers. Sandwiches here are an in-between size, as all start with a half or quarter slice of bread. Some are spread with butter or margarine, others, with mayonnaise, thick salad dressing or prepared sandwich spread—clear to the edges. Remove crusts, if you wish, but toppings should cover the bread completely! To be typically Danish, there would be only one of a kind on a tray, but you can fix one or many to suit your taste and time. A good rule of thumb is to allow two sandwiches for each guest. To fix ahead, spread bread, arrange in a single layer on a cookie sheet or tray lined with a damp towel; cover with wax paper, foil or transparent wrap; and chill. Prepare toppings too and chill separately. Notes with each recipe give special hostess' hints and tell how far ahead sandwiches can be made up. Here is your guide to the sandwiches shown in our picture.

1315

1. *Anchovy-Egg Squares.* 2. *Onion-Beef Foldovers.* 3. *Steak Sandwich Tartare.* 4. *Shrimp Pyramids.* 5. *Tomato-Cucumber Curlicues*

Anchovy-Egg Squares

Eggs with fish are a traditional choice. If you wish, vary with sardines or herring.

Spread thin slices of white or whole-wheat bread with butter or margarine, then with prepared mustard. Cut each slice into quarters; overlap 4 slices of hard-cooked egg, petal fashion, on each; sprinkle lightly with salt and pepper. Garnish each sandwich with two rolled anchovy fillets, each centered with a caper.
Note—One hard-cooked egg will give you 8 big neat slices, and a 2-ounce can of rolled anchovy fillets about 10. Make up only an hour ahead.

Onion-Beef Foldovers

Three favorites of men—pumpernickel, roast beef and crisp onion rings go into these zesty open-facers.

Spread slices of pumpernickel bread with butter or margarine, then lightly with prepared mustard; halve. Top each half with folded thin slices of cold medium-rare roast beef; garnish with crisp French fried onion rings. Season with freshly ground pepper.
Note—The thinner you slice the beef, the better it tastes. If you wish, crisp the onion rings (they come in a can) in a heated oven before serving. Sandwiches can be made about an hour ahead.

Steak Sandwich Tartare

To eat, mix egg yolk into lean raw meat, and season to your liking.

Scrape a piece of round steak, cut about 1 inch thick, with a knife or tablespoon to remove red meat from tissue. It will look like ground beef. (Or ask your meatman to put lean round steak through the grinder *twice*.) Spread square slices of dark rye bread with butter or margarine; cut in half, then spread with a thick layer of raw meat. Just before serving, wash, crack and separate a fresh egg for each sandwich, being careful not to crush shell. Return yolk to one half shell; set in middle of meat. (Use egg white to add to scrambled eggs for another meal.) Garnish each sandwich with shaved fresh horseradish or finely chopped green onion. Season with salt and pepper; add a dash of Worcestershire sauce or red pepper seasoning, if you wish.

1317

When it comes to buffets, the Danes really do them right. This super-buffet is a Smørrebrød for eight.
(See sketch on page 1315 for identification)

Note—Figure on 1 pound of meat for 8 sandwiches. Meat can be scraped 3 to 4 hours ahead, covered, and kept well chilled until ready to make up sandwiches, about a half hour ahead.

Shrimp Pyramids
Pile row upon row of tiny shrimps atop a half slice of bread spread with salad dressing.

Spread thin slices of white bread with mayonnaise or bottled coleslaw dressing; halve each. Arrange canned tiny cocktail shrimps, overlapping slightly, in a row along each long side of bread. Spoon a bit more mayonnaise or coleslaw dressing down middle; top with another row of shrimps; garnish with tiny sprigs of parsley. Sprinkle with lemon juice just before serving.
Note—It takes about 3 dozen tiny shrimps for each sandwich and you can count on about 90 perfect ones from a 3-ounce jar. Put sandwiches together about an hour ahead, if you wish.

Tomato-Cucumber Curlicues
"Salad" sandwiches rate high in popularity, look gay, and taste so refreshing.

Spread thin slices of white or rye bread with butter or margarine, then lightly with prepared sandwich spread; cut in half. Place 3 thin slices of tomato, overlapping, on top of each; garnish with 2 cucumber twists. Sprinkle with salt and pepper and dillweed, if you wish.
Note—To make cucumber twists: Slice an unpared cucumber thin, then cut each slice to center and twist. Make these sandwiches only a half hour ahead.

1318

Danish Appetizer Meat Balls
Guests pop these spicy little beef-and-pork balls into fluffy rolls to eat, finger style.
Makes 8 servings

    ¾ pound ground beef
    ¼ pound ground pork
    1 small onion, grated
    ½ cup fine dry bread crumbs
    1 teaspoon salt
    ¼ teaspoon pepper
    ⅛ teaspoon ground nutmeg
    ⅛ teaspoon leaf marjoram, crumbled
    2 eggs
    ½ cup milk
    3 tablespoons vegetable shortening
    1 can (10½ ounces) condensed beef consommé
    SAUCE PIQUANT (recipe follows)

1 Combine ground beef and pork with onion, bread crumbs, seasonings, eggs and milk in a medium-size bowl; mix lightly with a fork. Shape into 48 small balls.
2 Brown, a few at a time, in shortening in a large frying pan. Drain off all fat from pan; return meat balls. Pour consommé over; cover. Simmer 15 minutes, or until cooked through.
3 Remove meat balls with a slotted spoon; keep hot while making SAUCE PIQUANT.
4 To serve, pile meat balls into a chafing dish or heated serving bowl; pour hot sauce over; garnish with a frond of fresh dill, if you wish.
SAUCE PIQUANT—Pour all liquid from frying pan into a 1-cup measure; add water, if needed, to make 1 cup. Return to frying pan; heat to boiling. Blend 2 tablespoons flour with 3 tablespoons water until smooth in a cup; stir into hot liquid. Cook, stirring constantly, until sauce thickens and boils 1 minute; stir in 2 tablespoons sweet-pickle relish. Makes about 1 cup.

Golden Finger Rolls
These two-bite dainties are just the right size to go with the tiny meat balls.
Bake at 375° for 15 minutes. Makes 2 dozen

    ½ cup milk
    2 tablespoons vegetable shortening
    1 tablespoon sugar
    1 envelope active dry yeast
    ¼ cup very warm water
    2 teaspoons grated onion
    2¼ cups sifted all-purpose flour
    1 teaspoon salt
    1 egg
    2 tablespoons light cream or table cream

1 Scald milk with shortening and sugar in a small saucepan; cool to lukewarm.
2 Sprinkle yeast into very warm water in a large bowl. ("Very warm" water should feel comfortably warm when dropped on wrist.) Stir until

yeast dissolves, then stir in cooled milk mixture and onion.

3 Beat in 1 cup of the flour and salt until smooth, then beat in remaining 1¼ cups flour to form a soft dough.

4 Turn out onto a lightly floured pastry cloth or board; knead 3 minutes, or until smooth and elastic, adding only enough flour to keep the dough from sticking.

5 Place in a greased bowl; turn to coat all over with shortening; cover with a clean towel. Let rise in warm place, away from draft, 40 minutes, or until double in bulk.

6 Punch dough down; turn out onto lightly floured pastry cloth or board; divide into quarters, then each quarter in 6 small pieces. Shape each into an about-2-inch-long "finger;" place, 2 inches apart, on ungreased cookie sheets.

7 Cover with a clean towel; let rise in warm place, away from draft, 30 minutes, or until double in bulk.

8 Make 3 shallow cuts in top of each roll with scissors. Beat egg with cream in a cup; brush over rolls.

9 Bake in moderate oven (375°) 15 minutes, or until golden. Serve warm, split and buttered, if you wish.

Note—Rolls may be made ahead and reheated just before serving this way: Place in a paper bag; sprinkle *very lightly* with water; close bag tightly. Heat in moderate oven (350°) 10 minutes.

●

Party Cheese Platter
Simple or elaborate, it's always popular.

A variety of cheeses to nibble along with tiny crackers or to eat atop small rounds of bread rates high at any party—in Denmark or our own country. Make up a tray of your favorite kinds—as many or few as you wish—choosing mild and zesty, soft and firm to please every taste. No fancy arrangement is needed—just leave in wedges or blocks so everyone can cut off a piece to match his appetite.

Kraemmerhuse
These shattery cookie cones are usually heaped with cream and served with strawberry preserves. Or try fresh strawberries.
Bake at 425° for 3 minutes. Makes 18 cones

2 egg whites
4 tablespoons (½ stick) butter or margarine
¼ cup sugar
½ cup sifted all-purpose flour
  SNOWY VANILLA CREAM *(recipe follows)*
  Fresh strawberries

1 Beat egg whites until they stand in firm peaks in a small bowl.

2 Cream butter or margarine with sugar until fluffy in a medium-size bowl. Stir in flour, then fold in beaten egg whites, ⅓ *at a time,* until no streaks of white or yellow remain. (Be sure to fold in egg whites *slowly* so they'll stay fluffy-light.)

3 Drop batter, a rounded teaspoonful for each cone, on a well-buttered cookie sheet; spread into a 5-inch circle. (Make only two at a time, leaving about 2 inches between edges, as wafers must be rolled while hot.)

4 Bake in hot oven (425°) 3 minutes, or just until golden-brown around edge.

5 Loosen each from cookie sheet with a spatula but do not remove; pick up at edge with fingers, then roll quickly into a cone. (Hold one end loosely for top, twisting the other end to make a point.) Place, pointed end down in a bottle with a neck about 1 inch wide. (A baby bottle, milk, or salad-dressing bottle is just the right size.) Let stand 1 to 2 minutes, or until cool enough to hold its shape, then cool completely on a wire rack.

6 Repeat Steps 3, 4, and 5, cooling and buttering cookie sheet between each baking, to make 18 cones.

7 Fill cones generously with SNOWY VANILLA CREAM about 5 minutes before serving. (If filled further ahead, they will soften and lose their shape.) Stand cones upright in a generous mound of sugar in a pretty bowl; place on a large tray or platter. Frame bowl with strawberries. Set out dessert plates and forks for serving. Or place cones on serving plates and, in true Danish style, serve with a bowl of strawberry preserves for everyone to spoon on top of the cream.

SNOWY VANILLA CREAM—Beat 1 cup cream for whipping with 2 tablespoons 10X (confectioners' powdered) sugar and ½ teaspoon vanilla until stiff in a medium-size bowl. Makes enough to fill 8 cones.

Note—Cones keep perfectly for a week or more if packed carefully and stored in a container with a tight-fitting lid. For another special treat, bake cookies as flat rounds, then crumble and sprinkle over ice cream.

1319

This molded Baked Salmon Mousse with Poulette Sauce is every bit as delicate and velvety as it looks.

LUNCHES FOR ALL SEASONS

A GOURMET LUNCH FOR 6

1320

Watercress Frappé
Baked Salmon Mousse   Poulette Sauce
Duchess Potato Nests with Peas
Tossed Salad
Coconut Ice Cream Cake
Iced Coffee

Watercress Frappé
Pungent watercress and creamy potato soup
make this refreshing appetizer soup.
Makes 6 servings

1 can (2 to a package) dry cream of potato
  soup mix
½ bunch watercress

1 Prepare soup mix, following label directions;
cool slightly.
2 Wash and dry watercress; remove any coarse
stems, then chop remaining stems and leaves.
(There should be about 1 cup.) Stir into soup.
(Or, if you prefer, twirl soup in an electric
blender until creamy-smooth.) Chill in covered
container.
3 Pour into parfait glasses, dividing evenly.
Garnish each with a radish flower and parsley,
if you wish. (To make a radish flower, trim root
end and leafy top. Holding radish, root end up,
make deep cuts lengthwise with very sharp
knife, then turn radish and cut again at right
angles to first cuts. Chill in a bowl of ice and
water about 2 hours, or until "petals" open
slightly.)

Baked Salmon Mousse

Fish goes elegant when turned into this light fluffy loaf served with creamy shrimp sauce.
Bake at 350° for 1 hour. Makes 6 servings

    4 eggs
    1 can (1 pound) salmon
    2 tablespoons lemon juice
    ½ teaspoon salt
    ½ teaspoon Worcestershire sauce
    1 cup evaporated milk (from a tall can)
    2 tablespoons fine dry bread crumbs
      POULETTE SAUCE (recipe follows)

1 Separate eggs, placing 2 of the whites in a cup for next step, and 2 in a medium-size bowl for Step 4. Place the 4 yolks in a small bowl and set aside for POULETTE SAUCE.
2 Drain and flake salmon, removing any bones and skin. Combine salmon with 2 egg whites from cup, lemon juice, salt and Worcestershire sauce in large bowl; mash and beat with a fork until salmon is shredded completely. Cover; chill 45 minutes.
3 While salmon mixture chills, pour evaporated milk into an ice-cube tray; freeze until ice crystals form around edge. Spoon into chilled medium-size bowl; beat until stiff; keep cold.
4 Beat remaining 2 egg whites until they form soft peaks. Fold whipped evaporated milk, then beaten egg whites into chilled salmon mixture until no streaks of white remain.
5 Grease a 6-cup melon mold or 6-cup deep baking dish well; sprinkle with bread crumbs. Spoon salmon mixture into mold; set in a shallow baking pan; place on oven shelf. Pour boiling water into pan to depth of about 1 inch.
6 Bake in moderate oven (350°) 1 hour, or until a knife inserted deep into top comes out clean; remove mold from water; let cool 5 minutes. Loosen around edge with knife; invert onto heated serving platter.
7 Serve with POULETTE SAUCE; garnish with lemon and lime wedges, if you wish.

●

Poulette Sauce

Egg yolks from the salmon mousse add extra richness to this delicately seasoned topper.
Makes about 2 cups

    1 can (10 ounces) frozen cream of shrimp soup
    1 soup can milk
    1 teaspoon grated onion
    4 egg yolks (from BAKED SALMON MOUSSE)
    1 tablespoon lemon juice

1 Combine soup, milk and onion in medium-size saucepan; heat, stirring constantly, over medium heat until soup thaws and mixture is bubbly-hot. (Or heat in top of double boiler over hot water.)
2 Beat egg yolks slightly with a fork; stir in a generous ½ cup of hot soup mixture; quickly stir back into mixture in saucepan. Cook, stirring constantly, over low heat 3 minutes, or until sauce thickens slightly. Stir in lemon juice; season with salt and pepper to taste, if you wish. Serve hot.

●

Duchess Potato Nests

Rings of fluffy potatoes filled with cooked peas dress our fish platter in grand style.
Makes 6 servings

Watercress Frappé

1321

Coconut Ice-Cream Cake

This cream-frosted dessert gives you cake and ice cream all in one. It's a perfect make-ahead, too.

Makes one 10-inch cake

1 package orange-chiffon cake mix
2 pints strawberry ice cream
1 cup cream for whipping
2 tablespoons 10X (confectioners' powdered) sugar
1 teaspoon vanilla
Few drops red food coloring
¾ cup flaked coconut (from a 3½-ounce can)

1 Prepare and bake cake mix in a 10-inch tube pan, then cool, following label directions. Remove cake from pan; wash pan.
2 Slice cake crosswise into 3 even layers; return top layer to pan. (Set middle layer aside for another dessert or a snacktime treat.)
3 Spoon ice cream in an even layer over cake in pan; top with remaining cake layer. Cover pan with foil; freeze 24 hours, or until very firm.
4 About 2 hours before serving, beat cream, 10X sugar and vanilla until stiff in small bowl; fold in a few drops red food coloring to tint delicate pink.
5 Unmold cake onto chilled serving plate. Frost with whipped cream; sprinkle top and side with coconut. Return to freezer until serving time.
6 Slice into wedges with a sharp long-blade knife. Wrap any remaining cake in foil and store in freezer.

A SOUP-AND-SALAD LUNCH FOR 6

Chilled Chicken Cream
Finlandia Potato Tower
Buttered Toast Chunks
Melon Crescents
Coffee

Chilled Chicken Cream

Canned soup seasoned with celery seeds has a delightfully different flavor.

Makes 6 servings

1 can (10½ ounces) condensed cream of chicken soup
1 cup light cream or table cream
½ cup milk
1 teaspoon lemon juice
½ teaspoon celery seeds

1 Combine all ingredients in an electric-blender container; cover. Beat 1 minute, or until creamy-smooth. (Or beat slightly longer with an electric beater.) Chill.

For thin gourmets: two-tone Coconut Ice-Cream Cake.

1322

2 envelopes instant mashed-potato powder
2 eggs, beaten
4 tablespoons (½ stick) butter or margarine
1 package (10 ounces) frozen green peas, cooked, drained and seasoned

1 Prepare instant mashed potatoes, following label directions; beat in eggs and butter or margarine until fluffy-light. Heat, stirring constantly, over low heat until steaming-hot.
2 Spoon quickly into a pastry bag, and, using large star tip, press out into 12 nests on serving platter. (Or spoon mounds of potatoes onto platter and shape into nests with back of spoon.) Fill with seasoned hot peas.

2 Pour into mugs or cups. Garnish each with a celery-stick stirrer and serve with tiny croutons to sprinkle over, if you wish.

•

Finlandia Potato Tower
Build this he-man salad with layers of creamy potatoes, seasoned spinach, egg and tomato slices and crisp bacon.
Makes 6 servings

> 6 medium-size potatoes, cooked, peeled, and sliced
> 1½ teaspoons seasoned salt
> 8 slices bacon, cut in 1-inch pieces
>   Vegetable oil
> ¼ cup cider vinegar
> 1½ teaspoons sugar
> 1 teaspoon dry mustard
> ½ cup cream for whipping
> ½ pound fresh spinach
> 6 hard-cooked eggs, shelled and sliced
> 1½ cups sliced cherry tomatoes (about 1 pint)

1 Place potato slices in a single layer in a shallow baking pan; sprinkle with 1 teaspoon of the seasoned salt. (Remaining salt is for Step 3.)
2 Sauté bacon until crisp in a medium-size frying pan; remove and drain on paper toweling.
3 Pour bacon drippings into a 1-cup measure; add enough vegetable oil to make ½ cup. Stir in vinegar, sugar, mustard and remaining ½ teaspoon seasoned salt. Measure 6 tablespoonfuls into frying pan and set aside for Step 6.

4 Blend cream into remaining dressing in cup; pour over potato slices. Chill at least 30 minutes to season and blend flavors.
5 Cut stems and any coarse ribs from spinach; wash leaves, then dry well.
6 When ready to serve, heat dressing in frying pan just to boiling; turn off heat; but leave pan on range. Add spinach; toss until well coated.
7 Arrange a layer of potato slices on each of 6 individual serving plates; top each, building into a cone, with a layer each of spinach, egg and tomato slices and bacon.

A COOL SUMMER LUNCH FOR 6

Tomato-Salad Stacks
Cucumber-Relish Cups
Golden Sesame Chips
Lime Sherbet
Iced Coffee

Tomato-Salad Stacks
Build these jumbo knife-and-fork "sandwiches" with lots of macaroni and tuna salads between slices of rosy tomatoes.
Makes 6 servings

6 large tomatoes
2 heads Bibb lettuce

A Soup and Salad Lunch hits the spot on a 90° day.

1323

Tomato-Salad Stacks accompanied by a cucumber-relish cup and golden sesame chips.

2 pints macaroni-and-cheese salad (from the dairy case)
2 pints tuna salad (from the delicatessen counter)

1 teaspoon salt
1 teaspoon sugar
1 tablespoon cider vinegar
1 tablespoon vegetable oil

1 Peel tomatoes, if you wish; cut out stem ends. Cut each tomato into 4 thick slices, keeping slices in order. Separate lettuce leaves, wash and dry well on paper toweling.
2 Build each "sandwich" seven layers high, dividing fillings evenly, on a serving plate this way: Tomato slice, lettuce, macaroni salad, tomato slice, lettuce, tuna salad, tomato slice, lettuce and macaroni salad. Top with end slice of tomato. Garnish with a frond of a green onion, if you wish, and serve with CUCUMBER-RELISH CUPS and GOLDEN SESAME CHIPS.

1 Trim ends of cucumber, then cut cucumber into 6 about-1½-inch-long chunks; scoop out insides to form cups. (Set cut-out pieces and ends aside for next step.) Make even saw-tooth cuts around rim of each cup for a pretty edge, if you wish. Cover and chill until serving time.
2 Pare cucumber ends; chop along with cut-out pieces and radishes; place in a small bowl. Sprinkle with salt; toss to mix. Let stand about 30 minutes, then drain well.
3 Stir in sugar, vinegar and vegetable oil; spoon into cucumber cups.

1324

Cucumber-Relish Cups
How pretty they look! And they're a cool crisp touch for any salad plate.
Makes 6 servings

1 long slender cucumber
8 radishes, trimmed

Golden Sesame Chips
Such a snap to make with refrigerated rolls as your starter.
Bake at 375° for 10 minutes. Makes about 5 dozen

1 package refrigerated butterflake or flake rolls

2 tablespoons melted butter or margarine
2 tablespoons sesame seeds

1 Separate the 12 rolls, then split each into 5 or 6 rounds. (Buttery layers pull apart easily.)
2 Place in a single layer on one or two buttered large cookie sheets. Brush with melted butter or margarine; sprinkle with sesame seeds.
3 Bake in moderate oven (375°) 10 minutes, or until crisp and golden. Serve hot.

A LAST-MINUTE WARM-UP LUNCH FOR 6

Tomato-Salmon Pie-ettes
Crispy Cheddar Cubes
Celery Stalks   Carrot Curls
Lemonade

Tomato-Salmon Pie-ettes

Zippy aspic goes between salmon-rice-salad layers in crisp little pastry shells.
Bake shells at 425° for 10 minutes. Makes 6 servings

  TART SHELLS *(recipe follows)*
1 cup uncooked regular rice
¼ cup bottled Italian salad dressing
1 envelope unflavored gelatin
1¾ cups tomato juice
3 tablespoons lemon juice
½ teaspoon sugar
¼ teaspoon celery salt
  Few drops liquid red pepper seasoning

1 can (1 pound) salmon, drained, boned and flaked
¼ cup chopped green onions
½ cup mayonnaise or salad dressing
½ teaspoon curry powder

1 Make, bake and cool TART SHELLS.
2 Cook rice, following label directions; drain; place in a medium-size bowl. Drizzle Italian dressing over; toss to mix well. Chill at least an hour to season and blend flavors.
3 While rice chills, soften gelatin in ¾ cup of the tomato juice in a small saucepan. Heat, stirring constantly, just until gelatin dissolves; remove from heat.
4 Stir in remaining 1 cup tomato juice, 2 tablespoons of the lemon juice, sugar, celery salt and liquid red pepper seasoning. (Set remaining lemon juice aside for next step.) Chill 30 minutes, or until as thick as unbeaten egg white.
5 Fold salmon, green onions, mayonnaise or salad dressing, remaining 1 tablespoon lemon juice and curry powder into chilled rice mixture; spoon about ⅓ cup into each tart shell, pressing down to make an even layer. Fill shells with thickened tomato-gelatin mixture. Chill at least an hour, or until firm.
6 Just before serving, top each with a mound of remaining salmon salad. (A small ice-cream scoop makes a handy dipper, or mold with two spoons.) Garnish each with a twist of lemon and serve with CRISPY CHEDDAR CUBES *(recipe follows)*, carrot curls and cut spears of Belgian endive, if you wish.

1325

Tomato-Salmon Pie-ettes and Crispy Cheddar Cubes are make-aheads for a Last-Minute Warm-Up Lunch.

TART SHELLS—Make pastry with ½ package piecrust mix, following label directions, or use your own recipe for single-crust pie. Roll out, half at a time, ⅛ inch thick, on a lightly floured pastry cloth or board; cut each into three 6-inch rounds, using a saucer for pattern. Fit into 4-inch tart-shell pans, pressing firmly against bottoms and sides; trim overhang. Prick well all over with a fork. Bake in hot oven (425°) 10 minutes, or until golden; cool in pans on wire rack, then remove.

Crispy Cheddar Cubes

One bite of these hot crusty little cheese cubes just coaxes you into having another.
Makes about one dozen

1 egg
¾ cup fine dry bread crumbs
½ pound Cheddar cheese, cut into 1-inch cubes
Vegetable shortening or vegetable oil for frying
Paprika

1 Beat egg with 1 tablespoon of the bread crumbs in a small bowl. Place remaining bread crumbs in a pie plate.
2 Dip cheese cubes into egg mixture, then into bread crumbs to coat well.
3 Melt enough vegetable shortening or pour in vegetable oil to make a 3-inch depth in an electric deep-fat fryer or large saucepan; heat to 380°.
4 Fry cheese cubes, a few at a time, 1 minute, or until crisp and golden. Lift out with a slotted spoon; drain well on paper toweling. Keep warm until all are cooked then dust lightly with paprika. To serve, thread 2 cubes on a skewer, kebab style.

AN ELEGANT EASTER LUNCHEON FOR 8

Jellied Consommé Cup
Springtime Glazed Ham
Cherry Almond Sauce
Braised Endive Spears
Creamy Peas in Noodle Nests
Emerald Salad Molds
Strawberry Angel Ring

Jellied Consommé Cup

Lemon gives this shimmery appetizer an inviting tang.

1326

Springtime Glazed Ham with Cherry Almond Sauce.

Chill 3 cans (10½ ounces each) condensed beef consommé well (overnight is best) so it will form a soft jelly. Spoon into 8 small glass cups or thin glasses; top each with a lemon wedge and sprig of parsley. Serve with thin wheat wafers or your favorite snack crackers. Makes 8 servings.

Springtime Glazed Ham
Nothing looks quite as festive, or is easier to fix, than a handsomely glazed ham.

Buy a whole or half ham, butt or shank end, or a thrifty shoulder "picnic." Each will be labeled COOK BEFORE EATING or FULLY COOKED and either one will bake perfectly.

When making your choice, count on a minimum of ½ pound for each serving and you should have enough left over for at least one dividend dish. Bake ham according to label directions.

To glaze: remove ham from oven about 1 hour before it's done. If it has a thick skin on top (some hams come without it), cut it away from fat layer, then score fat into squares or diamonds. Cover top generously with your favorite glaze or with our BROWN SUGAR SPARKLE GLAZE *(recipe follows)*. Continue baking, basting often with drippings in pan, 1 hour, or until top is richly glazed. Let ham stand about 20 minutes before carving, as it slices better if allowed to cool just a bit.

BROWN SUGAR SPARKLE GLAZE—Mix 1 cup firmly packed brown sugar, 1 teaspoon dry mustard, ¼ teaspoon ground cloves and 2 tablespoons cider vinegar in a bowl. Makes enough to glaze a 10- to 15-pound ham.

1328

Cherry Almond Sauce
Its delicate fruit 'n' spice flavor blends perfectly with ham. Each plump cherry is stuffed with a whole almond.
Makes about 2 cups

  1½ cups water
   ½ cup cider vinegar
    1 cup firmly packed brown sugar
    2 teaspoons mixed pickling spices
   ⅛ teaspoon anise seeds
    1 jar (1 pound) maraschino cherries
    2 tablespoons cornstarch
    2 tablespoons butter or margarine

   1 can (about 5 ounces) whole blanched almonds

1 Combine water, vinegar, brown sugar, pickling spices and anise seeds in medium-size saucepan. Heat to boiling, then boil rapidly 10 minutes, or until syrup measures about 1 cup. Set aside for next step.
2 Drain syrup from cherries into 1-cup measure; add water, if needed, to make 1 cup. Blend 1 to 2 tablespoons into cornstarch until smooth in medium-size saucepan; stir in remaining syrup, then pour in brown-sugar syrup through strainer to remove spices.
3 Cook, stirring constantly, until sauce thickens and boils 3 minutes. Stir in butter or margarine.
4 Stuff an almond into each cherry; stir into hot sauce; heat just to boiling.

Braised Endive Spears
Do splurge on this gourmet vegetable. Buttery sauce is its only seasoning.

Wash 12 small stalks of Belgian endive; halve each lengthwise; arrange in single layer in large frying pan. Pour in water just to cover; add 2 tablespoons lemon juice and 1 teaspoon salt. (Make sure water completely covers endive as this keeps it white during cooking.) Cover; simmer 10 minutes, or just until tender when pierced with a fork; drain carefully so as not to break stalks. Melt in 4 tablespoons butter or margarine. Arrange endive on heated serving plates; spoon butter sauce over. Makes 8 servings.

Creamy Peas in Noodle Nests
Each serving is vegetable and garnish, as it looks like a gold-and-green crinkly flower.
Makes 8 servings

    3 cups (half an 8-ounce package) noodles
      Vegetable shortening for deep frying
    2 packages (10 ounces each) frozen peas
   ½ cup light cream or table cream
    4 tablespoons (½ stick) butter or margarine

1 Cook noodles in boiling salted water in large saucepan *just 5 minutes.* (They should be not quite tender.) Drain; rinse under running cold water; drain again, then spread out in a large flat pan.
2 Melt shortening to a depth of 2 inches in deep

heavy saucepan; heat to 375°. (Or use an electric fryer, following manufacturer's directions.)

3 Divide noodles into 8 equal-size portions. Drop, one portion at a time, from slotted spoon into hot fat. (It will bubble up immediately.) As noodles come to the top (you can see them through bubbling fat), gather toward one side of pan with spoon and shape into a round. (If any bits tend to stick to spoon, push off with a fork.) Hold with spoon for a few seconds, or just until firm enough to keep its shape. When golden-brown underneath, turn; fry just long enough to brown other side. (Each noodle nest takes less than 2 minutes to cook.) Let fat reheat to 375° between each frying.

4 Drain on paper toweling; keep warm in heated oven while cooking remaining noodle nests and peas. (Or make nests several hours ahead and reheat in slow oven [325°] for about 10 minutes before serving.)

5 Cook peas, following label directions; drain. Pour cream over; season with butter or margarine; heat just until cream is bubbly.

6 Place a noodle ring on each serving plate; spoon creamy peas over.

Emerald Salad Molds

Nippy sour cream layered between spring-crisp vegetables in sparkling lime gelatin doubles for dressing.
Makes 8 servings

1 package (6 ounces) lime-flavor gelatin
2 cups hot water
1½ cups cold water
4 to 6 radishes, sliced thin
¼ cup lemon juice
½ teaspoon salt
¼ teaspoon liquid red pepper seasoning
½ cup dairy sour cream
2 green onions, trimmed and sliced thin
2 small cucumbers, scored and sliced thin

1 Dissolve gelatin in hot water in 4-cup measure; stir in cold water; chill 1 hour, or until as thick as unbeaten egg whites.

2 Place eight 5-ounce custard cups or molds in shallow pan of ice and water before starting decorative layer. (This will speed setting. When you finish a layer in the last cup, the first cup should be sticky-firm enough to add the next layer.)

3 Spoon 1 tablespoon chilled gelatin into each cup; let set just until beginning to be sticky-firm, then arrange 5 or 6 radish slices, slightly over-

lapping, in gelatin in each cup to make a pretty top. Carefully spoon in 1 more tablespoon gelatin and let set until sticky-firm.

4 Stir lemon juice, salt and liquid red pepper seasoning into remaining gelatin in 4-cup measure. Measure out ½ cup and stir into sour cream in small bowl. Keep both of these gelatin mixtures at room temperature while filling molds.

5 Layer sour-cream mixture over radish layer in each cup, dividing evenly. When sticky-firm, carefully spoon in 2 tablespoons seasoned gelatin; let set. Arrange a layer of green-onion slices on top; let set again.

6 Stir any remaining green-onion slices into remaining seasoned gelatin; fill cups, dividing evenly. Remove cups from ice and water; chill until firm.

7 To serve, arrange a ring of cucumber slices, overlapping, on each serving plate. Unmold salads by first loosening around edges with a thin-blade knife, then dipping *quickly* in and out of a pan of hot water and inverting onto each cucumber ring.

●

Strawberry Angel Ring

Delicately soft meringue ring filled with ice cream floats on a creamy sauce.
Bake at 300° for 30 minutes. Makes 8 servings

Meringue Ring

3 egg whites
⅛ teaspoon salt
½ teaspoon cream of tartar
½ cup extra-fine granulated sugar
¼ teaspoon vanilla

Sauce

2 whole eggs
3 egg yolks (from meringue)
6 tablespoons sugar
½ cup milk
½ teaspoon almond extract
1 cup cream for whipping
1 quart strawberry ice cream
1 cup sweetened sliced strawberries

1329

1 Make meringue ring: Beat egg whites, salt and cream of tartar until foamy-white and double in volume in large bowl. (This will take about 5 minutes with an electric beater.) Beat in sugar, 1 tablespoon at a time, beating well after each, until sugar is completely dissolved and me-

For a very special Springtime Luncheon, serve Crab Roulade with Shrimp Sauce, Fluted Mushrooms.

ringue stands in firm peaks. (Count on another 15 minutes' beating here.) Beat in vanilla.

2 Spoon meringue into a buttered 4-cup ring mold; set in baking pan; place on oven shelf; pour in hot water to depth of 1 inch.

3 Bake in slow oven (300°) 30 minutes, or until dry on top. Cool in mold on wire rack; leave in mold until ready to serve. (Meringue ring can be made several hours ahead, then let stand at room temperature until ready to finish dessert.)

4 Make sauce: Separate whole eggs, putting whites into medium-size bowl, and combining yolks with other 3 in small bowl.

5 Beat whites until foamy-white and double in volume. Beat in 2 tablespoons sugar until meringue stands in firm peaks. Beat egg yolks until thick; beat in remaining 4 tablespoons sugar, milk and almond extract.

6 Beat cream until stiff in large bowl; fold in meringue and yolk mixtures until no streaks of white or yellow remain; chill.

7 When ready to serve, pour sauce into a large shallow serving bowl; loosen meringue ring around edge with knife and unmold onto sauce; fill center with scoops of ice cream; garnish with sliced strawberries.

A SPRINGTIME LUNCHEON FOR 6

Bouquet Strawberry Cup
Crab Roulade with Shrimp Sauce
Fluted Mushroom Kebabs
Buttered Peas
May Salad Tray
Olive Dressing
Angel Cake à la Mode
Coffee

Bouquet Strawberry Cup
Makes 6 servings

1 pint strawberries
1 can (about 14 ounces) frozen pineapple chunks
1 pint lime sherbet
10X (confectioners' powdered) sugar

1 Wash and hull strawberries; pick out 6 of the biggest and prettiest to save for garnish, then halve remaining.

2 Drain pineapple chunks and spoon into 6 sherbet glasses. Stand strawberry halves, tip end up, around pineapple, dividing evenly. Place a small scoop of lime sherbet in center.

3 Dip the 6 reserved whole strawberries in 10X sugar to coat well and stand on top of sherbet. For a dainty touch, circle base of each glass with a ribbon-tied bouquet of spring flowers.

Crab Roulade
It's a real scene-stealer with crab-salad filling inside a puffy omeletlike roll.
Bake at 325° for 40 to 45 minutes. Makes 6 servings

 4 tablespoons (½ stick) butter or margarine
½ cup sifted all-purpose flour
½ teaspoon salt
    Dash of cayenne
2 cups milk
4 eggs, separated
    CRAB SALAD (recipe follows)
    SHRIMP SAUCE (recipe follows)
    FLUTED MUSHROOM KEBABS (recipe follows)

1 Grease jelly-roll pan, 15x10x1; line with wax paper; grease paper; dust with flour.

2 Melt butter or margarine in medium-size saucepan; remove from heat. Blend in flour, salt and cayenne; gradually blend in milk until smooth.

3 Cook, stirring constantly, 1 minute, or until mixture boils and is very thick.

4 Beat egg whites until they form soft peaks in medium-size bowl. Beat egg yolks slightly in large bowl.

5 Beat hot mixture *very slowly* into egg yolks; continue beating until thoroughly blended. Fold in beaten egg whites until no streaks of yellow or white remain. Spread evenly into pan.

6 Bake in slow oven (325°) 40 to 45 minutes, or until golden-brown and top springs back when lightly pressed with fingertip.

7 Remove from pan this way: Loosen around edges with spatula; cover with wax paper or foil. Place a large cookie sheet or tray on top, then quickly turn upside down. Lift off pan; peel off wax paper.

8 Spoon CRAB SALAD evenly over omelet. (Use a slotted spoon to let any dressing drip back into bowl.) Starting at one end, roll up omelet, jelly-roll fashion, lifting wax paper as you roll to steady and guide it.

9 Lift roll onto heated serving platter with two wide spatulas; spoon about ½ cup hot SHRIMP SAUCE over; garnish with FLUTED MUSHROOM KEBABS. Cut roll into thick slices with a sharp knife. Serve remaining sauce in a separate bowl to spoon over. (If serving time is delayed, keep roll warm in heated oven.)

CRAB SALAD—Drain and flake 2 cans (about 7 ounces each) king crabmeat, carefully removing any bony tissue. Combine with 2 cups finely diced celery, ½ cup toasted slivered almonds, ½ cup mayonnaise, ¼ cup dairy sour cream, 1 tablespoon lemon juice and ½ teaspoon salt in medium-size bowl; toss lightly to mix. (If made

1331

ahead, remove from refrigerator and let stand at room temperature for 15 minutes before filling omelet.) Makes 4 cups.

SHRIMP SAUCE—Thaw 1 can (10 ounces) frozen cream of shrimp soup in top of double boiler over boiling water. Blend in ¼ cup milk; heat until bubbly-hot. Stir in 2 tablespoons chopped parsley. Makes 1½ cups.

FLUTED MUSHROOM KEBABS—Wash 6 large fresh mushrooms, cut off stems close to caps. With a sharp thin-blade knife, mark center of each cap. Starting here, make a curved cut about ⅛ inch deep to edge. Repeat around cap to make 8 evenly spaced cuts. Now make a second curved cut just behind each line, slanting knife in so you can lift out a narrow strip. (Cap will now spread open slightly when heated.) Melt 2 tablespoons butter or margarine over medium heat in small frying pan; place mushrooms, cut side down, in pan. Sauté 1 to 2 minutes, or until golden; turn; sauté 1 minute longer. Skewer each to CRAB ROULADE with a wooden pick threaded with 3 small pickled onions. Makes 6 servings.

May Salad Tray

It combines two springtime bests in a most inviting way.

This attractive salad-relish server filled with MARINATED ARTICHOKE HEARTS, ENDIVE CURLS, and OLIVE DRESSING adds a bright touch to any luncheon table. Everything can be fixed ahead, ready to set out at the last minute.

MARINATED ARTICHOKE HEARTS—Cook 1 package frozen artichoke hearts, following label directions; drain; place in pie plate. Pour ¼ cup thin French dressing over; let stand at room temperature at least an hour to marinate. Drain; arrange on serving tray; sprinkle with 1 pimiento, diced. Makes 6 servings.

ENDIVE CURLS—Halve 2 stalks of Belgian endive lengthwise; shred each lengthwise into long thin strips with sharp knife. Chill in a bowl of ice and water several hours, or until curled. Drain well; arrange on serving tray. Makes 6 servings.

OLIVE DRESSING—Blend 1 cup mayonnaise, ¼ cup chili sauce, ¼ cup chopped ripe olives, 1 diced hard-cooked egg, 1 teaspoon Worcestershire sauce and ½ teaspoon seasoned salt in small bowl; chill. Makes 1⅔ cups.

A MERRY MAY BUFFET LUNCH FOR 12

Party Ragout
Three-Greens Salad Bowl
Parsley-Mustard Dressing
Ripe-Olive Chop-Chop
Corn Piquant
Preserved Watermelon Rounds
Cheese Bread Round
Pink Crown Chantilly Torte
Coffee

Party Ragout

Two meats, lamb and veal, plus six vegetables go into this hearty springtime stew.
Makes 12 servings

    2 pounds lamb shoulder, cut in cubes
    2 pounds veal shoulder, cut in cubes
    1 Bermuda onion, sliced thin
    4 cups shredded lettuce
    1 tablespoon salt
    ¼ teaspoon pepper
    1 teaspoon leaf rosemary, crumbled
    3 envelopes instant chicken broth
      OR: 3 chicken-bouillon cubes
    4 cups hot water
   18 small new potatoes, pared
    3 pounds fresh peas, shelled (3 cups)
    4 medium-size yellow squashes, sliced
    1 pint cherry tomatoes, hulled
    1 tablespoon butter or margarine
    6 tablespoons cornstarch
    6 tablespoons cold water

1 Trim all fat from lamb and veal. Combine meats with onion, lettuce, salt, pepper and rosemary in heavy kettle or Dutch oven.
2 Dissolve instant chicken broth or bouillon cubes in hot water in 4-cup measure; pour over meats and vegetables; cover. Simmer 1 hour. Place potatoes on top; simmer 1 hour longer, or until meats and potatoes are tender.
3 About 15 minutes before stew is done, cook peas and squashes, covered, in boiling slightly salted water in separate medium-size saucepans just until crisply tender; drain. Sauté tomatoes in butter or margarine in medium-size frying pan, shaking pan often, 3 minutes, or just until skins pop. Keep all vegetables hot.
4 Smooth cornstarch and cold water to a paste in a cup; stir into hot stew. Cook, stirring constantly, until mixture thickens and boils 3 minutes.
5 Spoon meat and potatoes into a heated 12-cup serving dish; spoon squash slices, then peas, in rings on top; place tomatoes in center. Garnish with a sprig of fresh rosemary, if you wish.
Tips for the hostess—Cooking peas, squashes

and tomatoes separately and using to garnish your stew not only give it a party look but help prevent spillovers, since your kettle of meats and potatoes will be quite full. If your kettle is extra-large and you want to cook everything together, add peas and squashes during last 15 minutes of cooking time. Let tomatoes steam on top of stew for 5 minutes.

Three-Greens Salad Bowl
Hostess tips tell how to keep it coming, invitingly crisp and fresh.

Cut off any coarse leaves from 1 large head each of Boston or butter lettuce, romaine, and curly endive or chicory. Wash and drain well. Tear outside leaves into bite-size pieces; leave small inner leaves whole. Fill a large salad bowl with about half of the greens. Toss with about ¼ cup PARSLEY-MUSTARD DRESSING (recipe follows), or just enough to coat greens well. (Too much dressing tends to make salad soggy. See hostess tips below for care of greens.) Makes 12 servings.

PARSLEY-MUSTARD DRESSING—Combine 1 tablespoon chopped parsley, 2 teaspoons finely cut chives, 1 teaspoon salt, 1 teaspoon sugar, 1 teaspoon dry mustard, ½ teaspoon paprika and ⅛ teaspoon pepper in a 2-cup jar with tight-fitting lid. Pour in ¾ cup vegetable oil and ½ cup cider vinegar; cover. Shake well to mix; chill. Shake again just before tossing with greens. Makes about 1½ cups.
Tips for the hostess—For salad-bowl refills, store ready-to-dress greens in a large transparent bag in the refrigerator, then simply toss with dressing as needed.

Ripe-Olive Chop-Chop
It's a conversation-piece relish—and so pungently fresh-tasting with stew.
Makes about 5 cups

    3 cans (2¼ ounces each) chopped ripe olives
1½ cups finely chopped celery
    1 cup finely chopped dill pickle (about 4 medium-size)
    ½ cup finely chopped onion
    1 clove of garlic, minced
    1 can (2 ounces) anchovy fillets

½ cup vegetable oil
¼ cup wine vinegar or cider vinegar
¼ teaspoon pepper

1 Combine olives, celery, dill pickle, onion and garlic in a large bowl; toss lightly to mix.
2 Drain oil from anchovies into olive mixture; cut anchovies into tiny pieces and stir in with vegetable oil; vinegar and pepper; toss well to mix; cover.
3 Chill several hours or overnight to season and blend flavors.
Tips for the hostess—Make this relish ahead and plan on plenty, for some guests may eat as much as a half-cupful. It's that good.

Corn Piquant
Easy-fix tangy dressing turns canned corn into a zippy relish.
Makes about 4 cups

    1 teaspoon sugar
    ½ teaspoon salt
    ¼ teaspoon paprika
    ¾ cup vegetable oil
    ¼ cup cider vinegar
    1 tablespoon prepared horseradish
1½ teaspoons Worcestershire sauce
    2 drops liquid red pepper seasoning
    2 cans (12 or 16 ounces) whole-kernel corn, drained

1 Combine all ingredients, except corn, in a jar with tight-fitting lid; shake well to mix.
2 Pour over corn in medium-size bowl; toss lightly to mix. Cover; chill several hours or overnight to season and blend flavors.
Tips for the hostess—For help-yourself serving, spoon relish into its serving dish with as little dressing as possible.

1333

Cheese Bread Round
Each slice of this mellow moist bread tastes teasingly of mild cheese.
Bake at 350° for 50 minutes. Makes two 8-inch round loaves

1 cup milk
2 tablespoons sugar
3 teaspoons salt
1 tablespoon butter or margarine
1 envelope active dry yeast
1 cup warm water

5 cups sifted all-purpose flour
2 cups grated Swiss cheese (8 ounces)

1 Scald milk with sugar, salt and butter or margarine in small saucepan; cool just until warm.
2 Sprinkle yeast into warm water in large bowl. ("Warm" water should feel comfortably warm when dropped on wrist.) Stir until yeast dissolves; stir in cooled milk mixture.
3 Beat in 2 cups of the flour to form a smooth soft dough. Beat in cheese; gradually beat in remaining 3 cups flour to make a stiff dough.
4 Turn out onto lightly floured pastry cloth or board; knead until smooth and elastic, adding only enough extra flour to keep dough from sticking.
5 Place in greased bowl; turn to coat all over with shortening; cover with clean towel. Let rise in warm place, away from draft, about 1 hour, or until double in bulk.
6 Punch dough down; divide in half; knead each a few times. Shape each into a ball. Place in a greased 8x1½-inch round layer-cake pan. Cover; let rise again in warm place, away from draft, about 1 hour, or until double in bulk.
7 Bake in moderate oven (350°) 50 minutes, or until bread gives a hollow sound when tapped. Remove from pans; cool on wire racks. Slice in wedges.
Tips for the hostess—This bread is really rich enough to eat plain, but if you wish, serve with butter or margarine. Or try it this way: Spread cut sides of each wedge lightly with butter or margarine; re-form into loaf and wrap in foil. Heat in moderate oven (350°) 10 minutes.

Pink Crown Chantilly Torte
Cake layers with baked-on meringue are "frosted" with whipped cream and decked with rosy strawberries.
Bake at 350° for 30 minutes. Makes 12 servings

1 cup sifted cake flour
1 teaspoon baking powder
¼ teaspoon salt
½ cup (1 stick) butter or margarine
1¼ cups sugar
5 eggs, separated
1 teaspoon vanilla
3 tablespoons milk
¼ teaspoon almond extract
¾ cup toasted slivered almonds (from a 5-ounce can)

1334

A Merry May Buffet Lunch for a dozen close friends.

LUNCHES AND BRUNCHES

1 cup cream for whipping
2 tablespoons 10X (confectioners' powdered) sugar
2 cups (1 pint) strawberries, washed and hulled

1 Grease bottoms of two 8x1½-inch round layer-cake pans; dust lightly with flour.
2 Sift flour, baking powder and salt onto wax paper.
3 Cream butter or margarine and ½ cup of the sugar until fluffy in a medium-size bowl; beat in egg yolks, 1 at a time, beating well after each addition. (Save remaining ¾ cup sugar and egg whites for Step 5.)
4 Stir in vanilla and milk; blend in sifted flour mixture. Spread batter evenly into prepared pans.
5 Beat egg whites with almond extract until foamy-white and double in volume in a large bowl; sprinkle in saved ¾ cup sugar *very slowly*, 1 tablespoon at a time, beating all the time until sugar completely dissolves and meringue stands in firm peaks. (Beating will take about 25 minutes in all with an electric beater.) Spread over batter in pans; sprinkle with almonds.
6 Bake in moderate oven (350°) 30 minutes, or until meringue is golden.
7 Cool layers in pans on wire racks 5 minutes; loosen around edges with knife. Turn out, 1 at a time, onto palm of one hand; place on wire rack, meringue side up; cool completely.

Yes, Bouquet Crab Bowl is actually low in calories—just 149 per serving. Garnish is a crisp celery kebab.

8 Beat cream with 10X sugar until stiff in a medium-size bowl. Place each cake layer on a serving plate; spread with half of the whipped cream. Halve strawberries and arrange on top of cream. Cut each into 6 wedges.

Tips for the hostess—If weather is dry, these meringue-cake layers will hold well if made a day ahead. Just cool them completely, then wrap lightly in transparent wrap. When humidity is high, moisture in the air tends to make the meringue "weep." If you like, spread cream on layers about an hour ahead, then chill, ready to top with strawberries just before serving time.

FOR THE DIET CLUB: THREE LUSCIOUS LOW-CALORIE LUNCHES

MENU I
Bouquet Crab Bowl
Bran Puffins
Iced Tea
251 Calories Per Serving

Bouquet Crab Bowls
Makes 6 servings, 149 calories each

- 2 cans (about 7 ounces each) crabmeat
- 1 cup chopped celery
- ½ cup chopped sweet pickles
- 4 tablespoons low-calorie bottled French dressing
- 2 heads Boston lettuce, washed and separated into leaves
- 3 hard-cooked eggs, shelled

1 Drain crabmeat; flake and remove bony tissue, if any. Combine crab with celery and pickles in a medium-size bowl; drizzle with French dressing; toss lightly to mix; chill at least an hour to season.
2 When ready to serve, arrange lettuce leaves to form cups in individual salad bowls. Mound salad in center, dividing evenly.
3 Cut eggs in half lengthwise; scoop out yolks. Cut each white into thin strips and arrange, spoke fashion, over salad; press yolks through a sieve on top. Garnish each with celery slices threaded onto a kebab stick, if you wish.
   Dieter's serving: ⅔ cup salad, ½ egg, and ⅓ head lettuce.

Bran Puffins
Orange rind adds a new flavor spark to these two-bite muffins.
Bake at 400° for 15 minutes. Makes 30 tiny muffins, 34 calories each

- 1 cup sifted all-purpose flour

- 3 tablespoons sugar
- 1 teaspoon salt
- ¾ teaspoon baking soda
- ½ teaspoon baking powder
- 1 cup bran
- 1 teaspoon grated orange rind
- 1 egg
- 1 cup buttermilk
- 1 tablespoon butter or margarine, melted

1 Sift flour, sugar, salt, soda and baking powder into a medium-size bowl; stir in bran and grated orange rind.
2 Beat egg slightly with buttermilk and melted butter or margarine in a small bowl; add all at once to flour mixture; stir lightly just until evenly moist. (Batter will be lumpy.) Spoon into greased tiny muffin-pan cups to fill ⅔ full.
3 Bake in hot oven (400°) 15 minutes, or until golden; remove from cups. Serve warm.
   Dieter's serving: 3 muffins.

MENU II
Poached Shrimps with Lime Wedges
Hominy Timbales
Tomato Garni
Steamed Broccoli
Orange Cartwheel Salad
Coffee or Tea
300 Calories Per Serving

Poached Shrimps with Lime Wedges
Count on these favorites to rate high in popularity, low in calories.
Makes 4 servings, 155 calories each

- 2 pounds large fresh shrimps
- 1 tablespoon shrimp spice
   OR: 1 tablespoon mixed pickling spices
- 2 limes, cut into thin wedges

1337

1 Wash shrimps in cold water; peel off shells, but leave tails on. Make a shallow cut down back of each shrimp with a sharp-point knife; lift out the black line, or sand vein.
2 Half-fill a medium-size frying pan with water; season with shrimp or pickling spice; heat to simmering. Add shrimps; simmer 5 minutes, or just until tender; drain well.
3 Arrange, alternately, with lime wedges on serving plates.
   Dieter's serving: 8 shrimps and ½ lime.

Another low-calorie luncheon starring Tomatoes Garni.

Hominy Timbales

Even though you're watching calories, you can have a bit of butter or margarine.
Makes 4 servings, 94 calories each

2½ cups water
 ½ cup hominy grits
 ½ teaspoon salt
 2 teaspoons butter or margarine

1 Heat water to boiling in a small saucepan; stir in hominy grits and salt; cover. Cook, stirring several times, 40 minutes, or until very thick. Spoon into four *very lightly* buttered 5-ounce custard cups; let stand 10 minutes, then unmold.
2 Top each with ½ teaspoon butter or margarine. Garnish with parsley, if you wish.
 Dieter's serving: 1 timbale.

Tomatoes Garni

Onion, celery and green pepper give canned tomatoes a lively flavor boost.
Makes 4 servings, 72 calories each

 2 cans (1 pound each) canned whole tomatoes
 1 small onion, peeled and sliced
 ¼ cup chopped celery
 ¼ cup chopped green pepper
 1 teaspoon salt
 ⅛ teaspoon pepper
 Granulated or liquid no-calorie sweetener
 1 slice bread, toasted and cut into tiny cubes

1 Empty tomatoes carefully into a medium-size frying pan.
2 Stir onion, celery, green pepper, salt and pepper into frying pan; sweeten with your favorite no-calorie sweetner, using the equivalent of 1 teaspoon sugar. Heat just to boiling.
3 Lift out four of the prettiest tomatoes with a slotted spoon and place each in an individual serving bowl; spoon remaining over top. Sprinkle evenly with toasted bread cubes.
 Dieter's serving: 1 cup.

Orange Cartwheel Salads

Perfect for a meal starter too! Seasoner is a zippy blend of lemon and dill.
Makes 4 servings, 41 calories each

 ½ medium-size head iceberg lettuce
 2 medium-size seedless oranges

 ¼ cup lemon juice
 1 teaspoon dillweed
 Granulated or liquid no-calorie sweetener

1 Cut lettuce into 4 slices; place on salad plates. Peel oranges; cut each into 8 slices; arrange 4 each on top of lettuce.
2 Mix lemon juice, dillweed and your favorite no-calorie sweetener, using the equivalent of 2 teaspoons sugar, in a cup; drizzle over oranges.
 Dieter's serving: 1 slice lettuce, 4 slices orange, and 1 tablespoon dressing.

MENU III
Fruit-Crowned Ham Steak
Snowcap Carrot Nest
Herbed Zucchini
Garden Relish Plate
Coffee or Tea
423 Calories Per Serving

Fruit-Crowned Ham Steak

Most any dieter will be satisfied with a big slice of mustard-glazed meat, plus a peach half and pineapple ring.
Bake at 350° for 1 hour. Makes 4 servings, 290 calories each

1 slice ready-to-eat ham (about 1 pound)
1 can (1 pound) diet-pack peach halves
 Whole cloves
4 slices diet-pack pineapple (from a 1-pound, 4-ounce can)
1 tablespoon prepared mustard

1 Trim all fat from ham; score edge of slice so that it will lie flat during cooking; place in a shallow baking dish.
2 Drain syrup from peaches into a cup; stud 4 of the peach halves with whole cloves. (Save remaining peaches for dessert another day.) Arrange peach halves and pineapple slices around ham.
3 Stir mustard into peach syrup; pour over ham and fruits.
4 Bake in moderate oven (350°), basting several times with syrup in dish, 1 hour, or until ham and fruits are lightly glazed. To serve, cut ham into 4 even-size pieces; top each with a peach half and pineapple slice, cut and twisted, on serving plates. Garnish with watercress, if you wish.
 Dieter's serving: ¼ of the ham, ½ peach, and 1 slice pineapple.

Snowcap Carrot Nests

Serving trick: Ricing potatoes and carrots, then combining them, makes a little go far.
Makes 4 servings, 79 calories each

10 medium-size carrots, pared and sliced thin
 1 teaspoon salt
½ teaspoon leaf marjoram, crumbled

A third low-calorie luncheon, this one features a Fruit-Crowned Ham Steak at 290 calories a serving.

½ cup water
2 medium-size potatoes, pared and cut up

1 Combine carrots with salt, marjoram and water in a medium-size saucepan; cover.
2 Simmer 20 minutes, or until tender; drain, then shake pan over low heat to dry slices.
3 Cook potatoes, covered, in a small amount of boiling salted water in a small saucepan 15 minutes, or until tender; drain, then shake pan over low heat the same as carrots.
4 Put carrots through a ricer; spoon into rings on serving plates. Repeat ricing with potatoes; spoon into carrot rings.
   Dieter's serving: ½ cup carrots and ¼ cup potatoes.

1340

Herbed Zucchini

It takes only a smidgen of butter with herbs and bouillon to season this vegetable most invitingly.
Makes 4 servings, 45 calories each

4 medium-size zucchini
¼ cup water
1 envelope instant chicken broth
  OR: 1 chicken-bouillon cube
1 tablespoon butter or margarine
1 teaspoon mixed salad herbs

1 Trim ends of zucchini and quarter each lengthwise, then cut into 3-inch-long sticks. Combine with remaining ingredients in a medium-size frying pan.
2 Heat to boiling, crushing bouillon cube, if using, with a spoon; stir well to mix; cover.
3 Cook 15 minutes, or until zucchini is crisply tender.
   Dieter's serving: ¾ cup.

Garden Relish Plates

A dieter may even enjoy seconds, as the calories are so low.
Makes 4 servings, 9 calories each

2 stalks Belgian endive
12 radishes

1 Quarter endive; cut each quarter into thin strips almost to core end. Place in a bowl of ice and water.
2 Trim radishes; cut four thin "petals" in each from tip almost to stem; fold "petals" back carefully so as not to break; cut center part into eighths. Chill in a bowl of ice and water.
3 When ready to serve, drain both vegetables well; arrange on salad plates.
   Dieter's serving: ½ stalk endive and 3 radishes.

A PICTURE PORTFOLIO OF PARTY TABLES PERFECT FOR LUNCHES AND BRUNCHES

Setting a buffet table correctly is as much science as art. The point is to line up the plates, silver, napkins, main courses, accompaniments and beverages in a logical sequence so that guests don't have to backtrack as they serve themselves. To keep the table uncrowded, set the centerpiece nearby.

Colors are miracle workers as this gaily dressed table proves. The napkins repeat the red of the tablecloth print, the mauve place settings the lovely lavender-blue of the anemone arrangement.

Flowerpots aren't for live flowers alone. They make nifty holders for aluminum foil arrangements that you can speedily snip out with scissors.

Table settings should change with the seasons, reflecting through choice of color and centerpiece the mood of a particular time of year. This table dressed in warm shades is appropriately autumnal.

For an arrangement of marigolds, a uniquely textured vase. It's actually a small melon.

Asparagus escapes the saucepan and ends up fencing in flowers.

SHOWPIECE CENTERPIECES FOR
LUNCHES AND BRUNCHES

1344

You needn't be an expert to create flower, fruit and vegetable arrangements that will reap compliments for your party tables. And a flower-filled garden, wonderful as it is to have, isn't a necessity either. Many of our arrangements require only a few flowers, available at your florist's, along with the inexpensive floral equipment, you'll find so helpful. For the necessary fruits and vegetables, simply head for the nearest supermarket.

**HOW TO MAKE
VEGETABLE/FRUIT BOUQUETS**

There is no need to search for fancy flower containers when you can use fruits and vegeta-

bles. We used melons, oranges and eggplants (pumpkin and squash work well, too). Simply scoop out a small section from the top, large enough to hold a container. We used plastic medicine bottles in the oranges, a plastic cottage-cheese container in the watermelon, and jelly glasses in the rest. Cut the flower stems in varying lengths and arrange them casually, with the tallest ones in the center and bits of leather-leaf fern or other green garden foliage at the base, as shown in the photos. For the asparagus container, we straight-pinned asparagus upright around a cardboard paint bucket (a disposable ice bucket can also be used). Any garden or hot house flowers can be substituted for those shown.

Helpful Hints
1 Always cut flower stems at an angle, using a knife; do not break stems or cut with scissors.

For a big table, a big bouquet in a big vase—a watermelon, for example.

What lovelier for anemones than a shiny, scooped-out, plump, deep purple eggplant?

2 Check water in containers twice a day and keep containers filled.

3 To keep bouquets fresh-looking longer, recut stems every other day.

4 Consider where you are going to place your arrangement and be sure that it looks equally well from all sides.

5 If fruit containers don't stand straight, slice a small section off the bottom.

6 For some of the larger arrangements, you may want to insert a spiked flower holder in the container.

7 For the asparagus and carnation arrangement we used a block of Styrofoam (or floral clay) which had been thoroughly soaked in water for 10 minutes. If you use a cardboard paint bucket, insert another container inside it, as the water could soak through. A plastic cottage-cheese container, plastic food-storage container or a child's sand pail would all work.

1345

LUXURIOUS

LEFTOVERS

LUXURIOUS LEFTOVERS:
WAYS TO USE UP TURKEY AND CHICKEN, PORK, HAM AND TONGUE, BEEF, VEAL AND LAMB

Ham on hand? A refrigerator or freezer full of turkey? Tag ends of chicken or meat or vegetables? Of course. Everyone has them. The problem every cook faces is what to *do* with them. How to disguise these leftovers so that the family isn't *aware* of eating up the turkey or ham or whatever.

It's easier than you think. The best policy is to *plan* for leftovers at the time you shop. How many of your favorite recipes *begin* with diced cooked turkey or chicken, with cubed or minced ham? Take a look. No point in roasting a turkey, stewing a chicken or baking a ham for that one favorite recipe. But, when you're planning a turkey dinner, also plan for one or two other favorite recipes by buying a big enough bird. The same practice works with nearly all meats.

Leftover vegetables, rice and pasta are trickier to cope with because, frankly, they *are* best the first time around. Still, they can be slipped into casseroles and salads, soups and stews with imagination and success.

In the following pages you'll find some of FAMILY CIRCLE's most ingenious leftover recipes. *Planned*-overs, they should be called, because they have been carefully worked out to make the most of meats and vegetables, thereby pampering both the family and the food budget.

◀ *This is a leftover? It is. Leftover turkey at that. To give the dish its proper name, Turkey Alfredo.*

WHAT TO DO WITH LEFTOVER TURKEY AND CHICKEN

Turkey Alfredo
Cheese-seasoned noodles, breaded and browned slices of cooked turkey, and a rich saucy topping make this Continental treat.
Makes 4 servings

1 package (8 ounces) regular noodles
1 cup freshly grated Parmesan cheese
½ cup (1 stick) butter or margarine
   SUPREME SAUCE (recipe follows)
1 egg
1 teaspoon leaf oregano, crumbled
½ teaspoon salt
   Dash of pepper
2 tablespoons water
¾ cup fine dry bread crumbs
8 slices roast breast of turkey
3 tablespoons olive oil or vegetable oil

1 Cook noodles in a kettle, following label directions; drain; return to kettle. Add Parmesan cheese and 5 tablespoons of the butter or margarine; toss lightly with two forks until butter or margarine melts and noodles are evenly coated. Keep hot. (Remaining butter or margarine is for Step 4.)
2 While noodles cook, make SUPREME SAUCE; set aside for Step 5.

1347

3 Beat egg with oregano, salt, pepper, and water in a second pie plate; place bread crumbs in a second pie plate.

4 Dip turkey slices into egg mixture, then into bread crumbs to coat well. Brown slices, a few at a time, in the remaining 3 tablespoons butter or margarine mixed with olive oil or vegetable oil in a large frying pan.

5 Spoon hot noodles into an 8-cup shallow broilerproof dish; arrange turkey slices, overlapping, on top; spoon SUPREME SAUCE over middle of turkey slices.

6 Broil, 4 inches from heat, 5 minutes, or until sauce puffs and turns golden.

Supreme Sauce
Whipped cream folded into the sauce adds the gourmet touch.
Makes about ¾ cup

  2 tablespoons butter or margarine
  2 tablespoons all-purpose flour

  1 envelope instant chicken broth
    OR: 1 chicken-bouillon cube
½ cup milk
¼ cup cream for whipping

1 Melt butter or margarine in a small saucepan; stir in flour and chicken broth or bouillon cube. Cook, stirring constantly and crushing cube, if using, with a spoon, just until bubbly.

2 Stir in milk; continue cooking and stirring until sauce thickens and boils 1 minute; remove from heat.

3 Beat cream until stiff in a small bowl; fold into sauce.

Turkey Hawaiian
Pineapple, almonds and crisp vegetables turn cooked turkey into this showy tempter.
Makes 6 servings

  1 large onion, chopped (1 cup)
  2 tablespoons vegetable oil

*Another clever way to use up the big bird
—in Turkey Hawaiian with lots of pineapple.*

1 package (10 ounces) frozen peas
1½ cups sliced celery
2 envelopes instant chicken broth
  OR: 2 chicken-bouillon cubes
¾ cup water
2 tablespoons cornstarch
1 tablespoon soy sauce
1 can (about 14 ounces) pineapple tidbits
1 can (3 or 4 ounces) sliced mushrooms
1 can (5 ounces) water chestnuts, drained
  and sliced
½ cup whole blanched almonds
3 cups julienne strips of cooked turkey
  Fluffy hot rice

1 Sauté onion in vegetable oil just until soft in large frying pan.
2 Stir in frozen peas, celery, instant chicken broth or bouillon cubes and water. Cover; heat to boiling; simmer 5 minutes.
3 Blend cornstarch and soy sauce until smooth in 2-cup measure. Drain and stir in syrup from pineapple and liquid from mushrooms. Stir into vegetable mixture. Cook, stirring often, until sauce thickens and boils 3 minutes.
4 Stir in pineapple, mushrooms, water chestnuts, almonds and 2 cups of turkey. (Save remaining 1 cup for topping.) Cover; heat slowly until hot.
5 Spoon hot rice in a ring on heated serving plates; mound turkey mixture in center; top with saved turkey strips, arranged crisscross fashion. Garnish with sliced kumquat and crystallized ginger.

Turkey Stroganoff
Heat cooked turkey in a no-fuss creamy sauce for this quickie with a Continental flavor.
Makes 4 to 6 servings

1 large onion, chopped (1 cup)
2 tablespoons butter or margarine
2 to 3 cups julienne strips of cooked turkey
1½ cups turkey gravy
  OR: 1 can (about 11 ounces) chicken gravy
2 tablespoons catsup
1 cup dairy sour cream
  Parsley noodles

1 Sauté onion in butter or margarine just until soft in large frying pan. Stir in turkey, turkey or chicken gravy and catsup; simmer 5 minutes.
2 Stir in sour cream; heat *just to boiling*. Serve over hot noodles tossed with chopped parsley.

Skillet Turkey Scramble
Turkey and ham go with rice, tomatoes and seasonings in this top-of-the-range winner.
Makes 6 servings

1 medium-size onion, chopped (½ cup)
1 clove of garlic, minced
2 tablespoons butter or margarine
1 teaspoon salt
½ teaspoon chili powder
⅛ teaspoon pepper
  Dash of cayenne
1 bay leaf
2 cans (1 pound each) stewed tomatoes
2 cups diced cooked turkey
1 can (8 ounces) chopped ham sticks, diced
  OR: 2 cups diced cooked ham
1 cup uncooked regular rice
1 tablespoon chopped parsley

1 Sauté onion and garlic in butter or margarine just until soft in large frying pan. Stir in seasonings, then remaining ingredients; cover.
2 Simmer, stirring often, 40 minutes, or until rice is tender and liquid is absorbed. Remove bay leaf.

Turkey Cassoulet
A popular French casserole inspired this inviting way with turkey.
Bake at 350° for 1½ hours. Makes 6 servings

1 pound (2 cups) large dried lima beans
4 cups water
1 can (about 1 pound) tomatoes
6 slices bacon
1 cup grated raw carrots
1 large onion, chopped (1 cup)
2 teaspoons salt
1 teaspoon leaf thyme, crumbled
1 teaspoon leaf basil, crumbled
1 bay leaf
¼ teaspoon pepper
2 cups diced cooked turkey
1 cup chopped celery
¼ cup whole-fruit cranberry sauce

1 Combine lima beans and water in large kettle. Heat to boiling; cover; cook 2 minutes. Remove from heat; let stand 1 hour.
2 Stir in tomatoes, bacon slices, carrots, onion and seasonings; cover. Heat to boiling; simmer 1 hour, or until skins of beans burst when you blow on a few in a spoon.
3 Lift bacon slices from beans and save for next step; remove bay leaf. Stir turkey, celery and cranberry sauce into beans; pour into 10-cup baking dish; cover.
4 Bake in moderate oven (350°) 1 hour. Un-

1349

cover; crisscross saved bacon slices on top. Bake 30 minutes longer, or until liquid is absorbed.

●

Turkey Salad Bake
Bake at 450° for 10 minutes. Makes 4 servings

2 cups finely crushed potato chips (about a 4-ounce package)
½ cup grated sharp Cheddar cheese
½ cup chopped walnuts
1 tablespoon butter or margarine
2 cups cubed cooked turkey
2 cups thinly sliced celery
2 teaspoons grated onion
¼ teaspoon salt
2 tablespoons lemon juice
½ cup mayonnaise or salad dressing

1 Mix potato chips and cheese in small bowl; pat half of mixture into bottom of a shallow 6-cup baking dish. (Save remaining for topping in Step 3.)
2 Sauté walnuts in butter or margarine in small frying pan, stirring often, 15 minutes, or until lightly toasted; drain on paper toweling. Toss with remaining ingredients in medium-size bowl.
3 Spoon into prepared baking dish; sprinkle saved potato-chip mixture on top.
4 Bake in very hot oven (450°) 10 minutes, or until hot and golden.

Tureen Turkey Treat
Hearty with vegetables and meat, it's a most inviting warmer-upper on a brisk day.
Makes 6 generous servings

SAVORY TURKEY BROTH (recipe follows)
¼ pound salt pork, diced
1 large onion, chopped (1 cup)
3 cups diced raw potatoes
1 cup diced celery
½ teaspoon salt
⅛ teaspoon pepper
1 can (about 1 pound) cream-style corn
1 large can (14½ ounces) evaporated milk
1½ cups diced cooked turkey
½ teaspoon leaf marjoram, crumbled
½ teaspoon leaf thyme, crumbled

1 Make SAVORY TURKEY BROTH and set aside for Step 3.
2 Sauté salt pork until crisp in kettle; push to one side. Add onion; sauté just until soft.

1350

3 Stir in potatoes, celery, salt, pepper and saved broth; cover; simmer 20 minutes, or until potatoes are tender.
4 Stir in corn, evaporated milk, turkey and seasonings. Heat just to boiling. Ladle into heated soup bowls or plates.
SAVORY TURKEY BROTH—Break turkey carcass to fit into a kettle. Add 1 sliced onion, 1 sliced carrot, handful of celery tops, 1 tablespoon salt, ¼ teaspoon pepper and 6 cups water; cover. Heat to boiling, then simmer 1 hour. Lift out carcass and, when cool enough to handle, remove and dice any bits of meat. Place in small bowl; cover and chill until ready to make soup. Strain broth into medium-size bowl; then chill enough to skim fat from top. Add water, if needed, to make 6 cups.

●

Turkey Puffs
How the ladies will rave over these! Golden popovers are halved and filled with turkey salad lightly seasoned with curry.
Bake popovers at 400° for 50 minutes. Makes 6 sandwiches

3 eggs
1 cup milk
1 cup sifted all-purpose flour
½ teaspoon salt
6 slices bacon
6 leaves Boston lettuce
CURRIED TURKEY SALAD (recipe follows)

1 Beat eggs just until foamy in a medium-size bowl; add milk, flour and salt all at once; beat briskly ½ minute. Scrape down side of bowl; beat 1½ minutes longer. (Batter will be thin and smooth.)
2 Pour into 6 well-greased 6-ounce custard cups, filling each ⅔ full. Set cups, not touching, in a shallow pan.
3 Bake in hot oven (400°) 50 minutes, or until puffed and golden-brown; remove from cups. Poke a small hole in side of each to let steam escape; cool on a wire rack.
4 Sauté bacon until almost crisp in a large frying pan; roll each slice around the tines of a fork to make a curl; drain on paper toweling.
5 Cut popovers in half lengthwise; line half of each with lettuce, then fill with CURRIED TURKEY SALAD, dividing evenly. Garnish with bacon curls and serve with remaining popover halves.

Curried Turkey Salad
Makes about 6 cups

    4 cups cubed cooked turkey
    2 tablespoons minced onion
    2 cups chopped celery
    1¼ cups mayonnaise or salad dressing
    1 teaspoon curry powder
    1 teaspoon sugar
    1 teaspoon salt
    2 teaspoons lemon juice
    2 teaspoons grated onion

1 Combine turkey, minced onion and celery in a large bowl.
2 Blend mayonnaise or salad dressing, curry powder, sugar, salt, lemon juice and grated onion in a small bowl; spoon over turkey; toss to mix well. Chill.

Turkey Tetrazzini
Bake at 425° for 20 minutes. Makes 6 servings

    1 package (8 ounces) thin spaghetti
    1 small onion, chopped (¼ cup)
    2 tablespoons butter or margarine
    2 tablespoons all-purpose flour
    1 envelope instant chicken broth
      OR: 1 chicken-bouillon cube
    1 teaspoon salt
    1 teaspoon dry mustard
    ½ teaspoon pepper
    1 large can (14½ ounces) evaporated milk
    1 can (3 or 4 ounces) sliced mushrooms
    2 pimientos, diced
    3 cups diced cooked turkey
    1 cup (¼ pound) grated sharp Cheddar cheese
    ¼ cup grated Parmesan cheese

1 Cook spaghetti, following label directions; drain; place in buttered 8-cup shallow baking dish.
2 While spaghetti cooks, sauté onion in butter or margarine until soft in large saucepan. Remove from heat; blend in flour, instant broth or bouillon cube, salt, dry mustard and pepper. Slowly stir in evaporated milk, then liquid from mushrooms plus water to make 1½ cups. Cook, stirring constantly, until sauce thickens and boils 1 minute; stir in mushrooms and pimientos.
3 Mix 2 cups sauce with drained spaghetti in baking dish, making a well in center to hold the turkey mixture.
4 Combine turkey with remaining sauce; spoon into dish with spaghetti; sprinkle cheeses on top.
5 Bake in hot oven (425°) 20 minutes, or until bubbly and golden. (If made ahead, cover lightly, cool, then chill until 30 minutes before

Turkey Puffs are bound to make a hit at a luncheon.

baking. If put into oven cold, allow an additional 15 to 20 minutes' baking time.)

1351

Avocado-Turkey Crown
Molded in two layers, it turns out with a shimmery avocado topping over a creamy turkey salad.
Makes 8 servings

Avocado Layer
    1 package (3 ounces) lemon-lime-flavor gelatin
    1 cup hot water
    ¾ cup cold water
    3 tablespoons lemon juice

When you're down to the tag ends of a turkey, it's time to make a sensational Avocado-Turkey Crown.

2 *drops liquid red pepper seasoning*
1 *avocado, halved, pitted, peeled and diced*

Turkey Layer

1 *envelope unflavored gelatin*
1 *envelope instant chicken broth*
   OR: 1 chicken-bouillon cube
½ *teaspoon salt*
½ *teaspoon dillweed*
5 *drops liquid red pepper seasoning*
1½ *cups water*
½ *cup mayonnaise or salad dressing*
2 *cups diced cold roast turkey*
½ *cup thinly sliced celery*
¼ *cup chopped walnuts*

1352

1 Make avocado layer: Dissolve lemon-lime gelatin in hot water in a medium-size bowl; stir in cold water, lemon juice and liquid red pepper seasoning.
2 Chill 1 hour, or just until as thick as unbeaten egg white; fold in diced avocado; pour into an 8-cup tube mold. Chill 30 minutes, or *just* until sticky-firm.
3 While avocado layer chills, make turkey layer: Soften gelatin with chicken broth or bouillon cube, salt, dillweed and liquid red pepper seasoning in water in a medium-size saucepan; heat, stirring constantly, just until gelatin and bouillon cube, if using, dissolve. Remove from heat.
4 Beat in mayonnaise or salad dressing until smooth; fold in turkey, celery and walnuts. Spoon over *sticky-firm* avocado layer. Chill at least 3 hours, or until firm. (Overnight is better.)
5 To unmold, run a sharp-tip thin-blade knife around top of mold, then dip mold *very quickly* in and out of a pan of hot water. Cover mold with a large serving plate; turn upside down, then carefully lift off mold. Garnish center with a few salad greens, if you wish. To serve salad, frame with MARINATED SQUASH RINGS *(recipe follows)*.

●

Marinated Squash Rings
Two kinds of squash, seasoned in French dressing, make a colorful border for Avocado-Turkey Crown.
Makes 8 servings

2 medium-size yellow squashes, washed, trimmed and cut into ¼-inch-thick slices

2 medium-size zucchini, washed, trimmed and cut into ¼-inch-thick slices

3 tablespoons thin French dressing

1 Cook squashes and zucchini together in boiling salted water in a large frying pan, covered, 5 minutes, or just until crisply tender; drain carefully. Place in layers in a pie plate, being careful not to break slices.

2 Drizzle French dressing over; cover. Let stand at room temperature about 1 hour to season and blend flavors.

Deep-Dish Chicken Pie

Not for dieters, but guaranteed to fill up a famished family.

Bake at 425° for 30 minutes. Makes 6 servings

6 medium-size potatoes, pared, quartered

6 medium-size carrots, pared and quartered

1 small onion, chopped (¼ cup)

¼ cup chopped green pepper

2 tablespoons butter or margarine

1 can (10½ ounces) condensed cream of chicken soup

3 cups chunks of cooked chicken (boiled, roasted, or broiled)

BISCUIT WEDGE TOPPING (recipe follows)

1 Cook potatoes and carrots in boiling salted water in large saucepan 15 to 20 minutes, or until tender; drain, saving 1 cup of liquid for next step.

2 While vegetables cook, sauté onion and green pepper in butter or margarine until soft in saucepan; stir in chicken soup and 1 cup saved liquid.

3 Spoon vegetables and chicken into 8-cup casserole; pour sauce over.

4 Bake in hot oven (425°) 15 minutes while making BISCUIT WEDGE TOPPING; arrange biscuits on top of hot mixture; bake 15 minutes longer, or until biscuits are golden.

BISCUIT WEDGE TOPPING—Sift 1½ cups sifted all-purpose flour, 2 teaspoons baking powder and ½ teaspoon salt into medium-size bowl; cut in ¼ cup (½ stick) butter or margarine; add ½ cup milk all at once; stir just until blended. Turn dough out onto lightly floured pastry cloth or board; knead lightly ½ minute; roll out to a 7-inch round; cut into 6 wedges; brush tops lightly with milk; sprinkle with ¼ teaspoon poppy seeds.

Curried Chicken Leftover

This one is a whole meal in itself. Almonds and apple add texture.

Makes 4 servings

¾ cup precooked rice

½ cup chopped red apple

1 cup diced cooked chicken

¼ cup toasted slivered almonds

1½ teaspoons grated onion

⅓ cup mayonnaise or salad dressing

2 tablespoons table cream or light cream

1 tablespoon lemon juice

½ teaspoon curry powder

¼ teaspoon salt

¼ teaspoon sugar

1 Cook rice in a small saucepan, following label directions; cool to room temperature. Combine with apple, chicken, almonds and onion in a medium-size bowl.

2 Blend remaining ingredients in a cup; stir into rice mixture; chill. Just before serving, garnish with red apple slices, if you wish.

Kashmir Chicken Curry

Freeze this leftover chicken dish, then serve when the family least expects it.

Bake at 350° for 2¼ hours. Makes 4 servings

1 medium-size onion, chopped (½ cup)

1 cup thinly sliced celery

4 tablespoons butter or margarine

2 tablespoons all-purpose flour

2 teaspoons curry powder

1 can (10½ ounces) condensed chicken broth
Water

1½ teaspoons salt

2½ cups diced cooked chicken

4 cups hot cooked rice (about 1 cup uncooked)

1 To make curry sauce: Sauté onion and celery in butter or margarine until soft in a medium-size saucepan; stir in flour and curry powder. Cook, stirring constantly, until bubbly. Add chicken broth, ½ broth can of water and salt; continue cooking and stirring until mixture thickens and boils 1 minute; remove from heat; add diced cooked chicken.

2 Place hot cooked rice in a large bowl; stir in curry mixture until well blended. Spoon into lightly greased 6-cup freezer-to-oven baking dish.

3 Wrap baking dish tightly with heavy-duty aluminum foil with a double fold on top; seal; label; place in refrigerator until cold; freeze.

1353

4 To heat: Place foil-wrapped, still-frozen curry in cold oven. Set heat at moderate (350°). Bake about 2¼ hours, or until bubbly-hot.

Chicken à la King

Nobody remembers what king this creamy dish is named for, but people have loved it since time immemorial
Makes 4 servings

4 tablespoons (½ stick) butter or margarine
4 tablespoons all-purpose flour
2 tablespoons finely chopped onion
1 teaspoon salt
½ teaspoon Worcestershire sauce
2 cups milk
2 cups diced cooked chicken
¼ cup diced pimiento (about 2 pimientos)
1 can (3 or 4 ounces) sliced mushrooms

1 Melt butter or margarine in medium-size saucepan; remove from heat.
2 Blend in flour, onion, salt and Worcestershire sauce; stir in milk.
3 Cook over low heat, stirring constantly, until sauce thickens and boils 1 minute.
4 Stir in chicken, pimiento and mushrooms; heat through.
5 Serve over hot buttered rice or toast, if desired.

Chicken Croquettes

When you go to a little trouble with leftover meat, it becomes a whole new dish.
Makes 8 croquettes

2 cups coarsely ground cooked chicken
1 cup (about 2 slices) soft bread crumbs
2 eggs, well beaten
2 tablespoons plus ½ cup milk
1 tablespoon minced onion
1 tablespoon minced green pepper
½ teaspoon salt
¼ teaspoon leaf savory, crumbled
Dash of pepper
¼ cup finely chopped, blanched, toasted almonds
½ cup fine dry bread crumbs
Melted vegetable shortening, lard or vegetable oil to make a 3-inch depth in kettle
SILKY VELOUTÉ SAUCE (recipe follows)

1 Combine chicken, soft bread crumbs, eggs, 2 tablespoons milk, onion, green pepper, salt, savory, pepper and almonds in medium-size bowl; chill about 2 hours.

2 Shape into 8 cylindrical croquettes, each 1 inch in diameter; roll in fine dry bread crumbs; dip in ½ cup milk; roll again in crumbs; brush off loose crumbs.
3 Heat fat in deep heavy kettle to 365° or 375° (a 1-inch cube of bread will brown in about 1 minute).
4 Fry croquettes, 2 or 3 at a time, 2 minutes, or until golden-brown; drain on paper toweling.
5 Serve on heated platter with SILKY VELOUTÉ SAUCE.

Silky Velouté Sauce
Makes 2 cups sauce.

¼ cup (½ stick) butter or margarine
¼ cup sifted all-purpose flour
⅛ teaspoon pepper
1 can (10½ ounces) chicken consommé
¼ cup water
1 teaspoon lemon juice

1 Melt butter or margarine in small saucepan; remove from heat.
2 Blend in flour and pepper; gradually stir in consommé and water.
3 Cook over low heat, stirring constantly, until sauce thickens and boils 1 minute; stir in lemon juice. Serve hot.

Chicken Indienne
Makes 6 servings

2 envelopes unflavored gelatin
1 tablespoon sugar
1 teaspoon curry powder
3½ cups canned chicken broth
2 tablespoons lemon juice
⅓ cup chutney (from a 6-ounce bottle), finely chopped
4 cups diced cooked chicken
1 cup chopped celery

1 Soften gelatin with sugar and curry powder in 1 cup of the broth in a medium-size saucepan; heat, stirring constantly, just until gelatin dissolves; remove from heat. Stir in remaining 2½ cups broth.
2 Measure ½ cup of the gelatin mixture into a small bowl; set aside for next step. Stir lemon juice into remaining gelatin in saucepan. Chill about 50 minutes or until as thick as unbeaten egg white.
3 Stir chutney into gelatin in small bowl; pour

1354

into a 6-cup mold; chill about 30 minutes or just until sticky-firm.

4 Fold chicken and celery into thickened gelatin in saucepan; spoon over sticky-firm chutney layer in mold. Chill several hours, or overnight, until firm.

5 To unmold, run a sharp-tip thin-blade knife around top of mold, then dip *very quickly* in and out of a pan of hot water. Cover mold with serving plate; turn upside down; gently lift off mold. Garnish with leaves of Belgian endive, halved seedless grapes and flaked coconut, if you wish.

●

Chicken Egg Rolls
This favorite of the Orient goes together so easily at home. For a crisp jacket, fill rolls ahead and chill overnight.
Makes 6 servings, 2 rolls each

Filling
    1 large onion, diced (1 cup)
    1 cup thinly sliced celery
    1 teaspoon vegetable oil
    1 tablespoon soy sauce
    2 cups diced cooked chicken
Pancakes
    4 eggs
 1½ cups water
 1½ cups sifted all-purpose flour
    1 teaspoon salt
      Peanut oil or vegetable oil

1 Make filling: Combine onion, celery and vegetable oil in a small saucepan; cover. Cook over low heat 10 minutes, or until soft. Stir in soy sauce; pour over chicken in a medium-size bowl; toss to mix well. Let stand while making pancakes.

2 Make pancakes: Beat eggs with water until foamy in a medium-size bowl; beat in flour and salt just until smooth. (Batter will be thin.)

3 Heat an 8-inch frying pan slowly; test temperature by sprinkling in a few drops of water. When drops bounce about, temperature is right. Add about 1 teaspoon peanut oil or vegetable oil, tilting pan to cover bottom completely.

4 Pour batter, ¼ cup for each pancake, into pan. Bake 1 to 2 minutes, or until top appears dry and underside is golden. Lift out onto paper toweling to cool. (Only one side is baked.) Repeat with remaining batter, adding a little oil before each baking, to make 12 pancakes; cool each separately on paper toweling.

Chicken Indienne is a curry, all right, but it's a cool and shimmery mold with chutney sealed on top.

5 When ready to fill, spoon ¼ cup chicken mixture slightly off center on baked side of each pancake. Fold short end up over filling, then fold both sides toward center and roll up, jelly-roll fashion, to cover filling completely; fasten with one or two wooden picks. Place in a shallow dish; cover; chill overnight.

6 When ready to cook, heat a 1½-inch depth of peanut oil or vegetable oil to 400° in an electric skillet or deep heavy frying pan. Drop in chilled rolls, 2 or 3 at a time; fry, turning once, 5 to 8 minutes, or until golden. Drain on paper toweling. Keep rolls hot in warm oven until all are cooked. Remove picks; serve rolls plain or with a bottled sweet-sour sauce, if you like.

●

Pagoda Chicken Bowl
It's a delightfully creamy salad twist on popular chicken and noodles. An instant helper gives you a flying start.
Makes 4 servings

1 package (6 ounces) noodles with chicken-sauce mix and almonds
1 can (about 9 ounces) pineapple tidbits, drained
1 cup sliced celery
2 cups cubed cooked chicken
⅓ cup mayonnaise or salad dressing
¼ cup milk
¼ teaspoon curry powder
  Boston lettuce
  Radish slices

1 Prepare noodles with chicken-sauce mix, following label directions for top-range method; set almonds aside for Step 3. Spoon noodle mixture into a medium-size bowl; cool, stirring lightly several times, at room temperature.

2 Set aside several pineapple tidbits and celery slices for a garnish; stir remaining with chicken into noodle mixture. Blend mayonnaise or salad dressing, milk and curry powder in a cup; fold into noodle mixture. Chill at least 30 minutes to season.

3 When ready to serve, spoon into a lettuce-lined salad bowl; sprinkle saved almonds on top. Garnish with rows of radish slices and saved pineapple tidbits and celery threaded onto a wooden pick.

Short-Cut Clubs
Chicken salad and deviled ham make up this quickie version of a popular sandwich.
Makes 4 servings

1 cup diced cooked chicken
1 cup finely diced celery
¼ teaspoon salt
  Dash of pepper
2 tablespoons mayonnaise or salad dressing
12 slices white bread, toasted and buttered
1 can (4½ ounces) deviled ham
2 medium-size tomatoes, sliced thin
  Lettuce

1 Combine chicken, celery, salt, pepper and mayonnaise or salad dressing in small bowl; toss lightly to mix. (Fix chicken salad ahead, if you like, then cover and chill until ready to make sandwiches.)

2 Spread toast with deviled ham, then layer each of four slices this way: Chicken salad, toast, tomato slices and lettuce; top with remaining toast, deviled ham side down. Hold in place with wooden picks.

3 Cut each in quarters; garnish with ripe or green olives, if you wish.

Double Salad Jumbo
Luscious for luncheon: seasoned asparagus and carrots and crunchy chicken salad, perched on golden waffles.
Makes 6 servings

2 cups diced cooked chicken
1½ cups diced celery
1 tablespoon chopped parsley
½ teaspoon seasoned salt
¼ cup mayonnaise or salad dressing
1 can (1 pound) sliced carrots, drained
1 can (about 15 ounces) asparagus spears, drained
3 tablespoons bottled thin French dressing
12 frozen waffles
  Boston lettuce
  Pretzel sticks

1 Combine chicken with celery, parsley and seasoned salt in a medium-size bowl; fold in mayonnaise or salad dressing. Chill at least 30 minutes to season and blend flavors.

2 Place carrots and asparagus in separate piles in a shallow dish; drizzle French dressing over all. Chill at least 30 minutes to season.

3 Just before serving, toast waffles, following label directions; place 2 on each of 6 serving plates; top each with several leaves of lettuce.

4 Spoon ½ cup chicken salad on one waffle on each plate; arrange carrots and asparagus in bundles on remaining waffles. Garnish each plate generously with pretzel sticks.

Glazed Ham Loaf is so showy it's hard to believe it isn't the beginning of the ham instead of the end.

WHAT TO DO WITH LEFTOVER PORK, HAM AND TONGUE

Glazed Ham Loaf
So special and showy, it's almost like having a holiday dinner all over again.
Bake at 400° for 40 minutes. Makes 8 servings

6 cups ground cooked ham (1½ pounds)
2 medium-size carrots, grated (1 cup)
1 cup soft bread crumbs (2 slices)
1 cup mashed potato
2 eggs, slightly beaten
2 tablespoons chopped parsley
1 medium-size onion, chopped (½ cup)
1 tablespoon butter or margarine
2 teaspoons prepared mustard
½ teaspoon salt

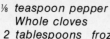

⅛ teaspoon pepper
Whole cloves
2 tablespoons frozen concentrated orange juice (from a 6-ounce can)
2 tablespoons honey
PINEAPPLE RELISH RINGS (recipe follows)

1 Combine ham, carrots, bread crumbs, potato, eggs and parsley in a large bowl; toss lightly to mix.
2 Sauté onion in butter or margarine just until soft in a small frying pan; stir in mustard, salt and pepper. Add to ham mixture; mix lightly.
3 Pack into a 6-cup melon mold or loaf pan, 9x5x3, rinsed with cold water; turn out into a greased shallow baking pan; stud top with whole cloves.
4 Mix concentrated orange juice and honey in a cup; brush half over loaf.
5 Bake in hot oven (400°) 20 minutes; brush with remaining orange-honey mixture. Bake 20 minutes longer, or until richly glazed.
6 Lift onto a heated serving platter; garnish with PINEAPPLE RELISH RINGS.
Note—While hot, this loaf is soft and may crumble somewhat when sliced

●

Pineapple Relish Rings
Popular canned pineapple goes gourmet-fancy.
Makes 8 servings

1 can (about 1 pound) sliced pineapple
¼ cup cider vinegar
1 teaspoon mixed pickling spices
2 tablespoons chopped parsley

1 Drain syrup from pineapple into a small saucepan; stir in vinegar and spices. Place pineapple in a small bowl.
2 Heat syrup to boiling, then simmer 5 minutes. Strain over pineapple; chill.
3 When ready to serve, drain pineapple slices well; roll edges in chopped parsley; arrange around ham loaf on platter.

1358

Easter Monday Dinner
Ham and colored eggs left over? Serve them this double-dividend way.
Makes 6 servings

2 cups diced cooked ham (about ¾ pound)
4 tablespoons (½ stick) butter or margarine

6 medium-size zucchini, trimmed and sliced ½ inch thick
4 tablespoons all-purpose flour
1 teaspoon dillweed
1 envelope instant chicken broth
1 tall can (14½ ounces) evaporated milk
½ cup water
6 hard-cooked eggs, shelled and quartered

1 Brown ham lightly in butter or margarine in a large frying pan; remove with slotted spoon and set aside for Step 4.
2 Stir zucchini slices into drippings in frying pan; cover. Cook over low heat, stirring several times, 20 minutes, or until zucchini is tender.
3 Sprinkle flour, dillweed and instant chicken broth over; stir lightly to mix, then stir in evaporated milk and water. Cook, stirring constantly, until sauce thickens and boils 1 minute.
4 Stir in browned ham, then place quartered eggs on top; cover. Heat slowly just until mixture is hot.

Alabama Ham Bake
Under a jumbo puffy-golden pancake are layers of mellow ham, sweet potatoes, and apples.
Bake at 375° for 1 hour. Makes 6 servings

2 medium-size sweet potatoes, pared and sliced thin
3 medium-size pears, pared, quartered, cored and sliced
3 cups diced cooked ham (about 1 pound)
3 tablespoons brown sugar
½ teaspoon salt
¼ teaspoon pepper
¼ teaspoon curry powder
⅓ cup apple cider
1 cup pancake mix
½ teaspoon dry mustard
1 cup milk
2 tablespoons melted butter or margarine

1 Layer half each of the sweet potatoes, pears and ham in an 8-cup baking dish.
2 Mix brown sugar, salt, pepper and curry powder in a cup; sprinkle half on top of layers in baking dish. Repeat with remaining sweet potatoes, pears, ham and seasonings; pour apple cider over; cover.
3 Bake in moderate oven (375°) 40 minutes, or until sweet potatoes are tender.
4 While ham mixture bakes, combine pancake mix, mustard, milk and melted butter or marga-

rine in a medium-size bowl, blending well to make a thin batter; pour over hot ham mixture.
5 Bake, uncovered, 20 minutes longer, or until pancake topping is puffed and golden.

●

Golden Gate Ham Rollups

Ham slices are wrapped around herb stuffing, then glazed and baked with peach halves.
Bake at 350° for 40 minutes. Makes 8 servings

2 *tablespoons minced onion*
2 *tablespoons butter or margarine*
¾ *cup water*
2 *cups ready-mix bread stuffing (half an 8-ounce package)*
8 *large thin slices cooked ham (about 1½ pounds)*
1 *can (1 pound, 13 ounces) peach halves*
½ *cup orange marmalade*
1 *tablespoon cider vinegar*
½ *teaspoon dry mustard*

1 Sauté onion in butter or margarine just until softened in medium-size saucepan. Add water; heat to boiling. Remove from heat; stir in bread stuffing.
2 Spoon about ¼ cup stuffing onto each ham slice; roll up; fasten with wooden picks, if needed. Place, seam side down, in single layer in greased large shallow baking pan.
3 Drain peach halves, saving ¼ cup syrup for next step. Place peaches, rounded side up, in baking pan with ham rolls.
4 Combine saved ¼ cup peach syrup, orange marmalade, vinegar and mustard in small saucepan; heat, stirring constantly, just until bubbly. Brush ham rolls and peaches with part of mixture.
5 Bake, uncovered, in moderate oven (350°), brushing often with remaining marmalade mixture, 40 minutes, or until richly glazed. Serve over hot buttered noodles, if you wish.

Cantonese Rollups

Makes 4 servings

3 *tablespoons vegetable oil*
2 *green onions, cut in ¼-inch pieces*
½ *cup finely diced cooked ham*
1 *can (about 1 pound) Chinese vegetables, drained*
2 *teaspoons soy sauce*
6 *eggs, slightly beaten*

1 Heat 1 tablespoon vegetable oil in me-dium-size frying pan; add onions and ham; cook 5 minutes.
2 Stir in Chinese vegetables and soy sauce; heat 2 to 3 minutes to blend flavors; keep hot while making omelets.
3 Heat ½ tablespoon oil at a time in small frying pan; pour in one fourth of the beaten eggs; cook over medium heat, just until top begins to set.
4 Cover with one fourth the hot vegetable mixture; continue to cook 2 to 3 minutes longer, or until golden-brown on bottom.
5 Fold in half; remove from pan; keep hot while making remaining 3 rollups. Serve with pre-served kumquats, Chinese noodles and for a spring touch, crisp green onions.

Tongue or Ham-and-Potato Scallop

Bake at 350° for 15 minutes. Makes 6 to 8 servings

6 *medium-size potatoes*
¼ *cup chopped green onions*
2 *tablespoons butter or margarine*
2 *tablespoons all-purpose flour*
1½ *teaspoons salt*
¼ *teaspoon pepper*
1 *cup milk*
½ *cup mayonnaise or salad dressing*
4 *teaspoons prepared mustard*
1 *teaspoon Worcestershire sauce*
1 *pound fresh peas, shelled (1 cup)*
6 to 8 *slices cooked tongue or ham*
1 *tablespoon white corn syrup*

1 Cook potatoes in boiling salted water in a large saucepan 45 minutes, or until tender; drain. Cool until easy to handle, then peel and slice; place in a large bowl; add green onions.
2 While potatoes cook, melt butter or margarine in a small saucepan; stir in flour, salt and pepper; cook, stirring constantly, just until bubbly.
3 Stir in milk; continue cooking and stirring until sauce thickens and boils 1 minute; remove from heat. Stir in mayonnaise or salad dressing, 3 teaspoons of the mustard and Worcestershire sauce. (Set remaining 1 teaspoon mustard aside for Step 7.)
4 Pour hot sauce over potatoes and onions; toss lightly until potatoes are coated. Spoon onto a large ovenproof platter or into an 8-cup baking dish.
5 Cook peas in boiling salted water in a small saucepan 5 minutes; drain.
6 Overlap tongue or ham slices in a ring on top of potatoes; spoon peas into center.
7 Mix corn syrup and remaining mustard in a cup; brush over tongue or ham.

1359

Two delicious ways to eat up ham: Tongue-or-Ham-Potato Scallop (foreground) and Ham-Macaroni Bake.

8 Bake in moderate oven (350°) 15 minutes, or until potatoes are hot and tongue or ham is lightly glazed. Garnish with strips of pimiento, if you wish.

•

Ham-Macaroni Bake
It takes just two cups of ham cubes for this generous casserole with a partylike topping.

Bake at 350° for 30 minutes. Makes 6 to 8 servings

1 package (8 ounces) elbow macaroni
1 small onion, grated
3 tablespoons butter or margarine
2 tablespoons all-purpose flour
1 teaspoon dry mustard
    Dash of pepper

2 cups milk
1 package (8 ounces) sliced Cheddar cheese
2 cups cubed baked ham
1 package (10 ounces) frozen South African
lobster tails
12 to 16 cherry tomatoes, washed and stemmed

1 Cook macaroni, following label directions; drain and keep hot for Step 4.
2 While macaroni cooks, sauté onion until soft in 2 tablespoons of the butter or margarine in a medium-size frying pan. (Set remaining 1 tablespoon butter or margarine aside for Step 7.) Stir in flour, mustard and pepper; cook, stirring constantly, just until bubbly.
3 Stir in milk; continue cooking and stirring until sauce thickens and boils 1 minute. Cut up half of the cheese slices; add to sauce, stirring until cheese is melted. Cut remaining cheese slices into 6 strips each.
4 Combine drained macaroni and ham in a buttered shallow 8-cup baking dish; pour cheese sauce over; arrange cheese strips, spoke fashion, on top.
5 Bake in moderate oven (350°) 30 minutes, or until bubbly-hot.
6 While casserole bakes, cook lobster tails, following label directions. Drain and cool until easy to handle. With scissors, cut through and remove the thick membrane on underside of shell. Take out lobster meat by peeling hard shell back with fingers of one hand and pulling meat toward you with the other. Place meat on cutting board; slice in half lengthwise with a sharp thin-blade knife.
7 Sauté lobster in saved 1 tablespoon butter or margarine in a medium-size frying pan 2 to 3 minutes, or until heated through; arrange on top of casserole. Sauté tomatoes in same pan 3 minutes, or just until skins start to pop; mound in center.

Ham-and-Apple Scallop

Jumbo pancake bakes crusty-golden atop ham and apples seasoned with sugar and spice. Bake at 350° for 1 hour. Makes 6 servings

3 cups diced ham
4 medium-size tart apples, pared, cored and
sliced
¼ cup firmly packed brown sugar
¼ teaspoon ground mace
¼ teaspoon pepper
¼ cup apple juice or water
1 cup pancake mix
1 cup milk
2 tablespoons melted butter or margarine

1 Make a layer of half of the ham and apples in an 8-cup baking dish.
2 Combine brown sugar, mace and pepper in a cup; sprinkle half over layer. Repeat with remaining ham, apples and sugar mixture. Pour apple juice or water over; cover.
3 Bake in moderate oven (350°) 40 minutes, or just until apples are tender.
4 Blend pancake mix, milk and melted butter or margarine to make a thin batter in medium-size bowl; pour over hot ham-apple mixture.
5 Bake, uncovered, 20 minutes longer, or until topping is puffed and golden.

●

Ham Sticks Hawaiian

Honey-and-fruit syrup glazes these colorful kebabs of ham, pineapple and green pepper. Makes 4 servings

1 can (about 13 ounces) pineapple chunks
4 tablespoons honey
2 tablespoons soy sauce
2 teaspoons lemon juice
2 teaspoons vegetable oil
24 one-inch cubes cooked ham
1 green pepper, seeded and cut into squares

1 Drain pineapple. Mix 4 tablespoons pineapple syrup with honey, soy sauce, lemon juice and vegetable oil in a cup.
2 Thread ham, pineapple chunks and green-pepper squares alternately onto 8 small skewers, dividing evenly. Place on broiler rack; brush lightly with honey mixture.
3 Broil 4 to 6 inches from heat 5 minutes; turn; brush again with honey mixture. Broil 5 minutes longer, or until hot and lightly browned.
4 Serve 2 kebabs each on a bed of buttered hot rice or noodles, if you wish.

●

Supper Potato Soup

Makes about 10 cups soup

6 medium-size leeks
1 large onion, chopped (1 cup)
3 tablespoons butter or margarine
8 cups water
6 peppercorns
1 bay leaf
1 ham bone
6 large potatoes, pared and quartered
¾ teaspoon salt
3 cups milk

1 Cut coarse tops and root ends from leeks; finely chop enough green ends to make ¼ cup; save for Step 7; coarsely chop remaining leeks.

1361

2 Sauté leeks and onion in butter or margarine in large kettle 8 to 10 minutes, or just until tender.

3 Add water, peppercorns, bay leaf and ham bone; cover; bring to boiling; reduce heat; simmer 1½ hours.

4 Add potatoes and salt; cook 20 minutes, or until potatoes are soft.

5 Remove ham bone; pick off any meat and chop; save for Step 7.

6 Sieve soup mixture through fine strainer into large bowl; chill; skim off any fat.

7 Combine soup mixture with milk and pieces of ham; heat *just* to boiling; add salt and pepper if needed; garnish with chopped leeks.

Easter-Monday Shortcakes

Have colored Easter eggs left? Team with chunks of ham in savory cream sauce to serve over onion biscuits.

Bake at 450° for 15 minutes. Makes 6 servings

Biscuits

    3 cups biscuit mix
    ½ cup sliced green onions
    1 cup milk
    2 tablespoons butter or margarine

Filling

    2 cups diced cooked ham
    6 tablespoons (¾ stick) butter or margarine
    6 tablespoons all-purpose flour
    ¼ teaspoon pepper
    1 teaspoon Worcestershire sauce
    1 envelope instant chicken broth
       OR: 1 chicken-bouillon cube
    3½ cups milk
    6 hard-cooked eggs, shelled and diced
    2 tablespoons chopped parsley

1 Make biscuits: Combine biscuit mix and green onions in large bowl; stir in milk with a fork to form a soft dough.

2 Drop half of dough into 6 equal-size portions on lightly greased cookie sheet; spread into 3-inch rounds. Slice butter or margarine into 6 thin pats; place 1 pat on each round; top with remaining dough, dividing and spreading evenly to seal in butter.

3 Bake in very hot oven (450°) 15 minutes, or until golden.

4 Make filling: Sauté ham lightly in butter or margarine in large saucepan; stir in flour, pepper, Worcestershire sauce and chicken broth

or bouillon cube; cook, stirring all the time, until mixture bubbles. Stir in milk slowly; continue cooking and stirring until sauce thickens and boils 1 minute. Fold in diced eggs and parsley; season with salt, if needed.

5 Split hot biscuits with a fork. (They'll come apart easily at their buttery layer.) Place on heated serving plates; fill and top with creamed-ham mixture, shortcake fashion.

Bonus Pea Soup

After most of the meat disappears, simmer every last bit of flavor from the bone for this old-time favorite.

Makes 6 to 8 servings

    1 ham bone
    8 cups water
    1 package (1 pound) dried split green peas
    4 medium-size carrots, pared and diced
    1 medium-size onion, chopped (½ cup)
    1 bay leaf

1 Combine all ingredients in large kettle; cover; simmer 1 hour, or until peas are soft.

2 Take out ham bone; cut off bits of meat and add to soup. Season, if needed, with salt and pepper; remove bay leaf. (Soup is thick, so thin with a little water, milk or tomato juice, if you wish.)

Pinwheel Ham-and-Corn Roll

Bits and pieces of ham and kernels of corn go into the filling for this supper loaf that bakes in a biscuit blanket.

Bake at 375° for 40 minutes. Makes 6 to 8 servings

    4 cups ground cooked ham (about 2 pounds)
    1 can (12 or 16 ounces) whole-kernel corn, drained
    1 cup soft bread crumbs (2 slices)
    2 eggs
    1 teaspoon mixed salad herbs
    ½ teaspoon dry mustard
    ⅛ teaspoon pepper
    ½ cup milk (for filling)
    2 cups biscuit mix
    ⅔ cup milk (for crust)
    PARSLEY CREAM SAUCE (recipe follows)

1 Combine ham, corn, bread crumbs, eggs, salad herbs, mustard, pepper and the ½ cup milk in a large bowl; mix lightly with a fork.

2 Prepare biscuit mix with the ⅔ cup milk, following label directions; turn out onto a lightly floured pastry cloth or board. Knead gently ½

1362

The secret ingredient of Easter Monday Shortcakes is—you guessed it—ham. It's diced and teamed with hard-cooked eggs in a nippy Worcestershire-spiked sauce and ladled in and atop quick-mix biscuits.

minute, then roll out to a rectangle, 18x12. Place on a lightly greased large cookie sheet.

3 Spoon ham filling down middle ⅓ of dough; fold edges up over filling to center; pinch together at top and ends to seal. Cut several slits in top to let steam escape.

4 Bake in moderate oven (375°) 40 minutes, or until crust is golden-brown. Cut in thick slices; serve with PARSLEY CREAM SAUCE.

Parsley Cream Sauce
Makes about 2 cups

1 small onion, chopped (¼ cup)
4 tablespoons (½ stick) butter or margarine
¼ cup sifted all-purpose flour
½ teaspoon salt
Dash of pepper
2 cups milk

1 envelope instant chicken broth
 OR: 1 chicken-bouillon cube
¼ cup chopped parsley

1 Sauté onion in butter or margarine until soft in a medium-size saucepan; stir in flour, salt and pepper; cook, stirring constantly, just until bubbly. Stir in milk and instant chicken broth or bouillon cube; continue cooking and stirring, crushing bouillon cube, if using, with a spoon, until sauce thickens and boils 1 minute.
2 Before serving, stir in parsley.

●

Jumbo Ham-and-Potato Roll
Bake at 425° for 30 minutes. Makes 6 servings

4 cups cut-up cooked ham
1 medium-size onion, peeled
2 medium-size potatoes, cooked, peeled and diced
2 eggs, slightly beaten
⅛ teaspoon pepper
½ cup milk (for meat loaf)
2 cups sifted all-purpose flour
1 teaspoon salt
⅓ cup vegetable shortening
⅔ cup milk (for crust)
 ZIPPY MUSTARD SAUCE (recipe follows)

1 Put ham and onion through food chopper, using coarse blade. Mix with potatoes, eggs, pepper and ½ cup milk in medium-size bowl; set aside for Step 4.
2 Sift flour and salt into medium-size bowl; cut in vegetable shortening with pastry blender until mixture is crumbly; blend in ⅔ cup milk with fork just until flour is completely moist—the same as for biscuits.
3 Turn dough out onto lightly floured pastry cloth or board; knead gently 5 or 6 times; roll out to a rectangle, 12x10.
4 Spoon ham mixture in loaf shape, 9x4, in center of pastry; fold pastry up over loaf; seal edges. Place, seam side down, on greased cookie sheet; cut several slits in top of pastry to allow steam to escape.
5 Bake in hot oven (425°) 30 minutes, or until pastry is golden-brown. Slice and serve with ZIPPY MUSTARD SAUCE.
 ZIPPY MUSTARD SAUCE—Blend ½ cup mayonnaise or salad dressing, ¼ cup dairy sour cream, 1 tablespoon prepared spicy brown mustard and ¼ teaspoon Worcestershire sauce in 1-cup measure. Makes about ¾ cup.

1364

Ham-and-Broccoli Royale
Bake at 350° for 45 minutes. Makes 8 servings

1 cup uncooked regular rice
2 packages (10 ounces each) frozen broccoli spears
6 tablespoons (¾ stick) butter or margarine
2 cups fresh bread crumbs (4 slices)
2 large onions, chopped fine (2 cups)
3 tablespoons all-purpose flour
1 teaspoon salt
¼ teaspoon pepper
3 cups milk
4 cups cubed cooked ham (1½ pounds)
1 package (8 ounces) sliced process white American cheese

1 Cook rice, following label directions; spoon into a greased refrigerator-to-oven baking dish, 13x9x2.
2 Cook broccoli, following label directions; drain well. Place in a single layer over the rice in baking dish.
3 Melt butter or margarine in a large frying pan; measure out 2 tablespoonfuls and sprinkle over bread crumbs in a small bowl; set aside.
4 Stir onions into remaining butter in frying pan; sauté until soft. Stir in flour, salt and pepper; cook, stirring constantly, until bubbly. Stir in milk; continue cooking and stirring until sauce thickens and boils 1 minute. Stir in ham; heat again just until bubbly; pour over layers in baking dish.
5 Place cheese slices over sauce; sprinkle buttered bread crumbs over all. Cover; chill.
6 About 45 minutes before serving time, uncover baking dish; place in moderate oven (350°).
7 Bake 45 minutes, or until bubbly and crumb topping is golden.

Eggplant-Ham Bake
Bake at 350° about 30 minutes. Makes 6 servings

1 medium-size onion, chopped
¼ cup chopped celery
¼ cup chopped green pepper
1 clove of garlic, halved
3 tablespoons butter or margarine
1 cup dairy sour cream
1 teaspoon salt
1 egg, slightly beaten
2 tablespoons milk
⅛ teaspoon pepper
¾ cup fine dry bread crumbs
1 medium-size eggplant, pared and cut into ½-inch slices

12 thin slices cooked ham
¼ pound Muenster or mozzarella cheese, thinly
   sliced

1 Sauté onion, celery, green pepper and garlic in butter or margarine just until tender; put into small bowl and remove garlic; slowly stir in sour cream and ½ teaspoon salt.
2 Combine egg, milk, ½ teaspoon salt and pepper in shallow dish; place bread crumbs in second dish.
3 Dip eggplant in egg mixture, then in crumbs; brown in a little hot fat, about 3 minutes on each side.
4 Line bottom of shallow oval baking dish, 12x7x2, with eggplant slices; cut 6 large slices in half; stand up around inside of dish.
5 Spread half of sour-cream mixture over eggplant in bottom of dish; top with 6 ham slices and half of the cheese; repeat layers; cover pan with foil.
6 Bake in moderate oven (350°) about 25 minutes, or until bubbly; uncover; bake 5 minutes to brown.

Ham-and-Lima Bake

1 pound (2 cups) large dried lima beans
4 cups water
2 teaspoons salt
1 cup grated raw carrots
4 slices bacon
2 cups cubed cooked ham
2 tablespoons vegetable oil
1 large onion, chopped (1 cup)
1 clove of garlic, minced
1 can (about 1 pound) tomatoes
¼ cup molasses

1 Cover lima beans with water in large kettle; heat to boiling; cover; cook 2 minutes. Remove from heat; let stand 30 minutes.
2 Reheat beans to boiling; add salt, grated carrot and bacon. (Do not cut slices.) Cover; cook 45 minutes, or until skins of beans burst when you blow on a few in a spoon.
3 While beans cook, brown ham lightly in vegetable oil in large frying pan. Push to one side of pan and sauté onion and garlic lightly; stir in tomatoes and molasses; cover; simmer 15 minutes.
4 Remove bacon from beans and save for next step. Stir ham mixture into beans; pour into a 12-cup baking dish; cover tightly.
5 Bake in slow oven (325°) 2 hours; remove cover; crisscross saved strips of bacon on top of casserole. Bake 1 hour longer, or until beans are tender. Makes 6 servings.

Luncheon Salad
Makes 6 to 8 servings

2 packages lemon-flavor gelatin
2 cups hot water
1½ cups apple juice
2 tablespoons lemon juice
2 teaspoons prepared horseradish
¼ teaspoon salt
½ small cucumber, unpared
¼ cup diced celery
¼ cup thinly sliced radishes
1½ cups diced cooked ham

1 Dissolve gelatin in hot water in medium-size bowl; stir in apple juice, lemon juice, horseradish and salt; chill until slightly thickened.
2 Cut cucumber lengthwise into quarters; remove seeds; cut crosswise into thin slices (makes about ½ cup).
3 Combine cucumber, celery, radishes and ham in medium-size bowl; fold into thickened gelatin.
4 Pour into 8-cup mold; chill 4 hours, or until firm.
5 Unmold onto serving plate; garnish with salad greens and radish roses, if desired; serve with your favorite salad dressing.

Crisscross Pork Braid
Hot-roll and Spanish-rice mixes, plus ready-cooked meat and vegetables really step up fixing time.
Bake at 400° for 15 minutes, then at 350° for 30 minutes. Makes 6 servings

1 package hot-roll mix
¾ cup water
1 egg
1 can (1 pound) cut green beans
¾ cup precooked Spanish-rice mix (from a 6-ounce package)
1 can (about 8 ounces) tomatoes
1 tablespoon butter or margarine
3 cups diced cooked pork
1 can (about 11 ounces) mushroom gravy
½ cup milk
2 tablespoons chopped parsley

1 Prepare hot-roll mix with water and egg and let rise once, following label directions.
2 While dough rises, drain liquid from beans into a 1-cup measure; add water, if needed, to make ¾ cup. Prepare Spanish-rice mix with tomatoes, butter or margarine and the bean

Any leftover pork roast? Crisscross Pork Braid gets it together with a Spanish rice mix, canned green beans and tomatoes and wraps them all up in a hot-roll-mix "pastry."

liquid, following label directions; stir in drained beans and pork.

3 Punch dough down; knead several times until smooth. Roll out to a rectangle, 16x14, on a lightly greased and floured cookie sheet. (Set cookie sheet on a damp towel to keep it from slipping.)

4 Spoon filling in a narrow strip down middle of dough, leaving about 2 inches at each end. Cut dough on each side into 1-inch-wide strips, cutting to within 1 inch of filling. Fold ends up over filling, then fold strips, alternating from side to side, at an angle across filling.

5 Brush all over with milk, if you wish, and wipe

any remaining flour from cookie sheet so it doesn't burn during baking.

6 Bake braid in hot oven (400°) 15 minutes; lower heat to moderate (350°). Bake 30 minutes longer, or until golden-brown and filling bubbles up.

7 While braid bakes, heat mushroom gravy and milk, stirring constantly, to boiling in a small saucepan; stir in parsley.

8 Cut braid into thick slices; serve with mushroom gravy to spoon over.

Ham-and-Shrimp Gumbo Salad

New Orleans popular soup inspired this rice-shrimps blend.

Makes 8 to 10 servings

1 cup uncooked regular rice
1 teaspoon sugar
½ teaspoon grated lime peel
2 tablespoons lime juice
1½ cups diced cooked ham (½ pound)
1 cup sliced celery
½ cup diced green pepper
1 package (12 ounces) frozen deveined shelled raw shrimps
1 package (10 ounces) frozen whole okra
6 tablespoons bottled thin French dressing
½ cup mayonnaise or salad dressing
1 tablespoon chopped parsley
1 cup halved cherry tomatoes
Romaine

1 Cook rice, following label directions; drain well. Place in a large bowl; stir in sugar, lime rind and juice, then ham, celery and green pepper.

2 Cook shrimps and okra in separate medium-size saucepans, following label directions, then drain well. (To garnish salad, set aside a few whole shrimps and whole okra pods.)

3 Dice remaining shrimps, but leave okra whole; add shrimps and okra to rice-ham mixture; drizzle French dressing over; toss to mix. Chill at least 30 minutes to season and blend flavors.

4 Just before serving, fold in mayonnaise or salad dressing, parsley and cherry tomatoes. Season to taste.

5 Spoon into a deep bowl lined with romaine; garnish with the saved shrimps and okra and a single whole cherry tomato.

Pizza Pork Pielets

Here meat-and-cheese filling is hidden inside a golden yeast crust.

Bake at 425° for 15 minutes. Makes 12 turnovers

1 package active dry yeast
1½ cups warm water
2 tablespoons vegetable oil

Who would guess that Pizza Pork Pielets are made of leftover pork (with an assist from pizza sauce mix)?

1367

2 cups sifted all-purpose flour
1 teaspoon salt
1 can (about 10 ounces) pizza sauce
2 cups diced cooked pork
1 package (6 ounces) mozzarella or pizza cheese, diced

1 Dissolve yeast in warm water in medium-size bowl; stir in vegetable oil; beat in flour and salt.
2 Turn out onto lightly floured pastry cloth or board; knead 10 times.
3 Place dough in greased medium-size bowl; cover with clean towel; let rise in warm place, away from draft, 30 minutes.
4 Punch dough down; roll out, half at a time, to a rectangle, 18x12, on lightly floured pastry cloth or board; cut into six 6-inch squares.
5 Stir pizza sauce into diced meat and cheese in medium-size bowl. Spoon about 2 tablespoons onto half of each square; fold dough over to make a triangle; press edges together firmly with a fork to seal. Press tops down lightly to spread filling evenly, then prick with fork to let steam escape; place on greased cookie sheet.
6 Bake in hot oven (425°) 15 minutes, or until golden-brown.
7 Serve hot, plain or with additional heated pizza sauce to spoon over, if you like.

California Pork Scallop
It bakes in layers of sweet pork slices and orange-seasoned stuffing.
Bake at 350° for 45 minutes. Makes 4 servings

1 large onion, chopped (1 cup)
4 tablespoons (½ stick) butter or margarine
1½ cups water
1 can (6 ounces) frozen concentrated orange juice
1 package (8 ounces) ready-mix bread stuffing (4 cups)
¼ teaspoon ground sage
8 slices cooked pork
¼ cup firmly packed brown sugar
½ teaspoon dry mustard
1 teaspoon Worcestershire sauce
1 can (about 11 ounces) chicken gravy

1 Sauté onion in butter or margarine just until softened in medium-size frying pan; stir in water and ¼ cup concentrated orange juice. (Save remaining ½ cup for Step 4.)
2 Heat to boiling; pour over bread stuffing and sage in medium-size bowl; stir to moisten well.

3 Alternate 3 layers of stuffing and 2 of pork slices, beginning and ending with stuffing, in greased 6-cup casserole.
4 Combine saved ½ cup concentrated orange juice, brown sugar, mustard and Worcestershire sauce in 1-cup measure; drizzle over top.
5 Bake in moderate oven (350°) 45 minutes, or until top is crusty-brown.
6 Heat chicken gravy in small saucepan; serve separately to spoon over scallop.

Stuffed Garden Peppers
Spaghetti-sauce mix and quick-cooking rice are the speedy helpers for this summer star.
Bake at 350° for 25 minutes. Makes 6 servings

1 medium-size onion, chopped (½ cup)
2 tablespoons vegetable oil
2 cups finely diced cooked pork
¾ cup packaged precooked rice
1 envelope spaghetti-sauce mix
½ teaspoon salt
1½ cups water
6 medium-size green peppers
1 cup (4 ounces) grated process American cheese

1 Sauté onion in vegetable oil in large frying pan just until softened. Stir in pork, rice, spaghetti-sauce mix, salt and water. Cover; heat to boiling; remove from heat; let stand 15 minutes.
2 Halve peppers lengthwise; cut out stems, seeds and membrane. Parboil in small amount boiling salted water in large saucepan 5 minutes; drain.
3 Arrange pepper halves in single layer in shallow baking dish; fill with meat mixture.
4 Bake in moderate oven (350°) 15 minutes; sprinkle grated cheese over; bake about 10 minutes longer, or until the cheese is melty.

Hot Pork 'n' Gravy Shortcakes
Heat pork slices in their own rich gravy, then spoon over piping-hot corn bread.
Bake at 400° for 30 minutes. Makes 6 servings

1 package corn-muffin mix
1 cup sifted all-purpose flour
½ cup sliced stuffed green olives
1 egg
Milk or water

1 package (10 ounces) frozen broccoli spears
4 medium-size carrots, pared and cut into thin sticks
12 slices cooked pork
1 can (about 11 ounces) chicken gravy

1 Combine corn-muffin mix, flour and olives in medium-size bowl. Beat egg slightly with milk or water called for in recipe on package for corn muffins plus ¼ cup more. Mix, following label directions. Pour into greased baking pan, 9x9x2.
2 Bake in hot oven (400°) 30 minutes, or until golden.
3 While corn bread bakes, cook broccoli, following label directions. Cook carrots in small amount boiling salted water in small saucepan 10 minutes, or until crisply tender; drain both vegetables well; keep hot.
4 Trim fat from pork slices; arrange in shallow baking dish; top with gravy. (If using canned gravy, blend in ½ cup water.) Cover; heat in oven with corn bread during last 15 minutes' baking.
5 Cut corn bread into serving-size pieces; top with hot pork slices and gravy, then broccoli spears and carrot sticks. Spoon more hot gravy over or serve separately.

Barbecued Pork Kebabs
Pork cubes and golden apricots threaded on skewers make this tempting dish.
Bake at 350° for 30 minutes. Makes 4 servings

1 cup dried apricots
1 cup boiling water
1 medium-size onion, chopped (½ cup)
2 tablespoons vegetable oil
½ cup apricot liquid
1 teaspoon bottled gravy coloring
1 tablespoon brown sugar
1 teaspoon salt
½ teaspoon curry powder
¼ cup vinegar
2 cups cooked lean pork cubes

1 Cook apricots in water 10 minutes, or just until softened in small saucepan; drain, saving ½ cup liquid for Step 2.
2 Sauté onion lightly in vegetable oil in small frying pan; stir in saved apricot liquid and seasonings; boil 1 minute to blend flavors.
3 Thread pork cubes and apricots alternately on skewers; place skewers, not touching, on a rack in shallow baking pan; brush with sauce.

4 Bake in moderate oven (350°), turning and basting two or three times with sauce, 30 minutes, or until richly glazed. Serve with boiled rice or mashed potatoes.

Supper Ham Salad
It's invitingly cool-looking with cubed ham, grapes and crunchy cucumber in a snowy dressing.
Makes 4 servings

2 cups cubed cooked ham
1 cup seeded halved green grapes
1 small cucumber, quartered lengthwise and sliced thin
4 radishes, trimmed and sliced thin
¼ cup mayonnaise or salad dressing
¼ cup dairy sour cream
1 head romaine

1 Combine ham, grapes, cucumber and radishes in a large bowl.
2 Blend mayonnaise or salad dressing and sour cream in a cup; fold into ham mixture; chill at least an hour to season and blend flavors.
3 Just before serving, line a salad bowl with romaine leaves; shred remaining into bottom. Spoon ham mixture into center. Garnish with a radish rose, if you wish.

Polynesian Pork Salad
Makes 6 servings

2 cans (1 pound, 2 ounces each) whole sweet potatoes, drained and cut into ¼-inch-thick slices
OR: 6 medium-size sweet potatoes, cooked, peeled and cut into ¼-inch-thick slices
5 tablespoons bottled Hawaiian dressing
1 can (about 1 pound) sliced pineapple, drained
2 cups cubed cooked pork
½ cup dairy sour cream
2 teaspoons honey
¾ teaspoon curry powder
1 head romaine
2 tablespoons cut chives

1 Place sweet potatoes in a large bowl; drizzle 4 tablespoons of the Hawaiian dressing over; toss lightly to mix; chill at least an hour to season and blend flavors.
2 Set 5 of the pineapple slices aside for garnishing salad in Step 5. Cut up remaining and mix with pork in a medium-size bowl.
3 Blend remaining 1 tablespoon Hawaiian

Cool leftovers: Supper Ham Salad
(center) and Tongue Saladettes.

Another cool way to use up leftovers: Polynesian Pork Salad.

dressing, sour cream, honey and curry powder in a cup; pour over pork-pineapple mixture; toss lightly to mix; chill.

4 Just before serving, line a salad bowl with romaine leaves; shred remaining into bottom. Place sweet-potato slices in a layer on top; spoon pork mixture in a mound in center.

5 Roll edges of saved pineapple slices in chives on wax paper; halve 3 slices and arrange in a ring around pork. Top pork with a whole pineapple slice; cut remaining slice in half; cut one half in half again and arrange on top, as pictured on page 1370.

Tongue Saladettes

Julienne strips of tongue and cheese frame cones of seasoned snowy rice dotted with peas and bits of pickle.
Makes 6 servings

    1 cup uncooked regular rice
    1 package (10 ounces) frozen peas
    ½ cup mayonnaise or salad dressing
    ½ cup chopped dill pickle
    1 teaspoon grated onion
    ½ teaspoon ground cumin
    2 heads Bibb lettuce
    3 cups julienne strips cold cooked tongue
    3 slices process American cheese (from an
      8-ounce package), halved and cut in thin
      strips

1 Cook rice in boiling salted water in a large saucepan, following label directions; drain; spoon into a large bowl.

2 Cook peas, following label directions; drain; add to rice.

3 Mix mayonnaise or salad dressing, pickle, onion and cumin in a small bowl; spoon over rice and peas; toss lightly to mix; chill.

4 Just before serving, line individual salad bowls with lettuce; mound rice mixture into cones in centers, dividing evenly. Pile tongue strips around edge; crisscross cheese strips on rice cones. Garnish with parsley, if you wish.

WHAT TO DO WITH LEFTOVER BEEF, VEAL AND LAMB

Sliced Beef Diane

Husky slices of beef simmer in a rich gravy sparked with peppy bottled savory sauce.
Makes 4 to 6 servings

    1 medium-size onion, sliced
    2 tablespoons butter or margarine
    8 to 12 slices cooked beef
    1 can (about 11 ounces) beef gravy
    2 tablespoons bottled savory sauce
    1 tablespoon Worcestershire sauce
    1 teaspoon salt

1 Sauté onion until softened in butter or margarine in medium-size frying pan; push to one side of pan. Brown beef slices, a few at a time; return all meat to pan.

2 Mix gravy with remaining ingredients in a 2-cup measure (thin with a tablespoonful or two of water if very thick); pour over meat; cover.

3 Heat to boiling; simmer 3 to 5 minutes to blend flavors. Serve with mashed potatoes or buttered rice.

French Beef Bake

Bake at 375° for 30 minutes. Makes 4 servings

    2 cups cubed roast beef
    2 tablespoons butter or margarine
    ½ teaspoon salt
    ½ teaspoon leaf thyme, crumbled
    ⅛ teaspoon pepper
    1 cup apple cider
    2 cans (1 pound each) white kidney beans,
      drained
    1 can (1 pound) small boiled onions, drained
    ½ cup chopped parsley

1 Brown beef in butter or margarine in a medium-size frying pan; stir in salt, thyme, pepper and cider; heat to boiling.

2 Spoon into a 6-cup baking dish; stir in beans and onions; cover.

3 Bake in moderate oven (375°) 30 minutes, or until bubbly-hot. Sprinkle with chopped parsley and serve with French bread, if you wish.

Roast-Beef Platter

Makes 6 servings

    4 tablespoons (½ stick) butter or margarine
    2 tablespoons prepared horseradish
    6 slices rye bread
    12 slices cold roast beef
    2 teaspoons finely chopped parsley
    6 lettuce wedges

Steak from leftover roast beef? Here's one way to do it—by making vinaigrette-topped Steak Parisienne.

1372

1 jar (about 1 pound) sliced pickled beets, well drained
2 cans (about 3 ounces each) potato sticks
Bottled coleslaw dressing

1 Blend butter or margarine with horseradish in small bowl; spread on bread.
2 Lay 2 slices of beef, overlapping, on each bread slice; sprinkle with parsley.
3 Arrange each open-face sandwich on a serving plate with a wedge of lettuce, beets and potato sticks. Serve with coleslaw dressing.

●

Chuck Wagon Beef Casserole
Beef and bacon, plus four vegetables, bake in a tarragon-seasoned sauce.
Bake at 350° for 30 minutes. Makes 6 servings

2 cups cubed cooked beef
3 tablespoons all-purpose flour
½ pound bacon (about 12 slices), cut in 1-inch pieces
1 can (10½ ounces) condensed beef broth
1 teaspoon paprika
1 teaspoon leaf tarragon, crumbled
1 can (about 1 pound) red kidney beans, drained
1 can (about 1 pound) chick peas, drained
1 can (12 or 16 ounces) whole-kernel corn, drained
1 cup chopped celery

1 Shake beef cubes with flour in a paper bag to coat evenly.
2 Sauté bacon until crisp in a large frying pan;

remove and drain on paper toweling. Pour off all fat, then return 2 tablespoonfuls to pan.
3 Add beef cubes and brown; remove. Stir any remaining flour into drippings in pan, then stir in beef broth, paprika and tarragon. Cook, stirring constantly, until mixture thickens and boils 1 minute.
4 Spoon beans, chick peas, corn and celery into a shallow 8-cup baking dish; top with browned beef cubes and bacon; pour sauce over.
5 Bake in moderate oven (350°) 30 minutes, or until bubbly-hot.

●

Steak Parisienne
Makes 4 to 6 servings

8 to 12 thin slices cooked beef
VINAIGRETTE SAUCE (recipe follows)
1 can (about 1 pound) Blue Lake whole green beans, drained
2 to 3 cups cooked sliced carrots
1 hard-cooked egg, chopped
Few thin slices Bermuda onion
8 to 12 cherry tomatoes

1 Arrange meat, overlapping slices, in center of large platter or chop plate; spoon half of VINAIGRETTE SAUCE over.
2 Arrange beans along one side of meat, carrots on other side. Stir egg into remaining sauce; spoon over vegetables.
3 Garnish platter with onion slices and cherry tomatoes. (This makes a handsome dish to make ahead, then chill. VINAIGRETTE SAUCE gives

an extra zip to both meat and vegetables on waiting.)

VINAIGRETTE SAUCE—Combine in jar with tight lid: ½ cup vegetable oil, ¼ cup wine or cider vinegar, 2 tablespoons chopped parsley, 1 teaspoon dry mustard, 1 teaspoon seasoned salt, 1 teaspoon sugar, ¼ teaspoon pepper and ¼ teaspoon paprika; shake to mix well. Makes about ¾ cup.

Deviled Beef Slices

Better make sure you have roast beef left for this treat—it's that good!
Makes 6 servings

1 egg
2 tablespoons prepared horseradish-mustard
1 cup onion-flavor cracker crumbs
6 slices roast beef
 Vegetable oil or vegetable shortening for frying

1 Beat egg with mustard in a pie plate; place cracker crumbs in a second pie plate. (For easy crushing, place crackers in a transparent bag and roll with a rolling pin.)
2 Dip beef slices into egg mixture, then into cracker crumbs to coat both sides well.
3 Fry in ¼-inch depth of hot vegetable oil or shortening in a large frying pan, turning once, 6 minutes, or until coating is crusty-golden.

Bonus Beef Pies

Bake at 375° for 45 minutes. Makes 4 servings

2 cups cooked beef cubes

¼ cup vegetable shortening
1 package frozen Italian green beans
1 cup sliced boiled potatoes
¼ cup gravy-thickening mix (from 14-ounce package)
2½ cups water
1 teaspoon salt
¼ teaspoon pepper
1 envelope onion-soup mix
1 package refrigerated bread sticks

1 Brown beef lightly in vegetable shortening in large frying pan; remove with slotted spoon, leaving fat in pan; arrange meat with green beans (thaw just enough to break apart) and potatoes in 4 individual casseroles, dividing evenly (or use one 6-cup casserole).
2 Blend gravy-thickening mix into fat in pan; stir in water, salt and pepper; heat to boiling; stir in onion-soup mix; lower heat; cook 3 minutes; pour over beef and vegetables in casseroles.
3 Bake in moderate oven (375°) 30 minutes.
4 Cut bread sticks in half crosswise; arrange 5 in spoke design on top of each casserole; bake 15 minutes longer, or until puffed and golden; garnish with parsley, if you wish.

Cartwheel Buffet Tray

With beef roasted ahead and ready to slice, and a bit of early-bird cooking, this sunny platter goes together fast.

Fix MIMOSA POTATO SALAD (recipe follows) in the morning and chill so it will unmold neatly. Drain canned whole Blue Lake green beans, drizzle with bottled French dressing, and slide them,

1373

Cartwheel Buffet Tray puts leftover roast beef in party dress.

LUXURIOUS LEFTOVERS

too, into the refrigerator to season. (You'll need just one 1-pound can for 8 servings.) To make the cheese rolls, buy long slices of caraway, Muenster, Swiss, Cheddar or any of your family's favorites, then simply roll up tightly, jelly-roll fashion. (Tip: Cheese rolls easily without cracking if it's slightly warm.) Just before serving, unmold potato salad in the center of a large tray. Drain beans, then wrap several inside each slice of roast beef; alternate beef and cheese rolls, spoke fashion, around edge of tray. Add a frilly garnish of endive or lettuce, if you wish.

Mimosa Potato Salad
Molded so easily in a bowl and garnished with sieved egg yolk, this favorite becomes a real show-off.
Makes 8 servings

6 *cups diced pared potatoes (about 6 me-dium-size)*
1 *medium-size onion, chopped (½ cup)*
1 *envelope instant beef broth*
  OR: 1 beef-bouillon cube
1 *cup water*
3 *hard-cooked eggs, shelled*
1½ *cups thinly sliced celery*
¼ *cup chopped parsley*
½ *cup mayonnaise or salad dressing*
1 *tablespoon cider vinegar*
1 *teaspoon salt*
¼ *teaspoon pepper*

1 Combine potatoes, onion, beef broth or bouillon cube and water in a medium-size saucepan; cover. Heat to boiling; cook 15 minutes, or just until potatoes are tender. Drain then shake pan gently over low heat to dry potatoes.

2 Halve eggs; remove yolks and set aside for Step 5. Dice whites and stir into potatoes along with the celery and parsley.
3 Blend mayonnaise or salad dressing, vinegar, salt and pepper in a cup; fold into potato mixture. Pack into a 6-cup bowl; chill several hours.
4 When ready to serve, loosen salad around edge with a knife; invert onto center of a large serving tray; lift off bowl.
5 Press saved egg yolks through a sieve; sprinkle all over salad mold. Garnish with a carrot-radish kebab, if you wish.

●

Country Beef Salad
A little beef plus macaroni turns into a just-hearty-enough supper dish.
Makes 6 servings

1 cup small macaroni shells (from a 1-pound package)
¼ cup sliced green onions
½ teaspoon salt
⅛ teaspoon pepper
1 tablespoon cider vinegar
1 tablespoon vegetable oil
2 cups cubed cooked beef
1 cup sliced celery
1 cup thinly sliced fresh broccoli flowerets (from a 2-pound bunch)
¼ cup mayonnaise or salad dressing
½ teaspoon sugar
1 teaspoon prepared horseradish
1 teaspoon prepared mustard
Iceberg lettuce

1 Cook macaroni shells, following label directions; drain; place in a large bowl. Stir in onions, salt, pepper, vinegar and vegetable oil; let stand about 1 hour to season and blend flavors.
2 Just before serving, stir beef, celery and broccoli into macaroni mixture. (Save stalks and remaining broccoli to cook as a vegetable for another meal.)
3 Blend mayonnaise or salad dressing, sugar, horseradish and mustard in a cup; fold into beef mixture. Spoon into a lettuce-lined salad bowl.

●

Old World Borsch Salad
Peasant-style beet soup prompted this hearty meat-and-potato salad.
Makes 4 to 6 servings

1 can (about 1 pound) small whole potatoes, drained
1 envelope instant beef broth
   OR: 1 beef-bouillon cube
1 can (about 1 pound) small whole beets, drained
2 tablespoons French dressing
4 cups finely shredded cabbage (about a 1-pound head)
½ cup sliced celery
1 small onion, diced
2 tablespoons sugar
1 teaspoon salt
¼ teaspoon pepper
1 cup (8-ounce carton) dairy sour cream
½ pound cooked corned beef, cut into thin strips
   Lettuce
   Caraway seeds

1375

Most gumbos and borsches are served in bowls. Ham-and-Shrimp Gumbo (front) and Old World Borsch (rear) are no exceptions—except that they're salads, not soups!

1 Combine potatoes with beef broth or bouillon cube in a small saucepan; add water to cover; heat to boiling. Remove from heat; cool in broth while mixing rest of salad.
2 Season beets with French dressing in a small bowl; chill.
3 Mix cabbage, celery, onion, sugar, salt and pepper in a large bowl; chill about 30 minutes.
4 Just before serving, drain cabbage and potatoes. Fold ¼ cup of the sour cream into cabbage; arrange with potatoes, beets and corned beef in separate mounds in a lettuce-lined large bowl. Spoon remaining sour cream into a lettuce cup; sprinkle with caraway seeds; set in center.

Molded Corned-Beef Ring
Three favorites—corned beef, cabbage and potatoes—go fancy in this summery salad.
Makes 6 servings

Corned-Beef Layer
2 envelopes unflavored gelatin
2 tablespoons sugar
3 cups water
2 beef-bouillon cubes
½ cup cider vinegar
2 cups diced cooked corned beef
2 cups chopped celery
¼ cup chopped green pepper
1 tablespoon prepared horseradish

Potato-Salad Layer
4 cups diced, peeled, cooked potatoes
2 cups finely shredded cabbage
1 small onion, chopped (¼ cup)
¼ cup chopped parsley
½ cup mayonnaise or salad dressing
½ cup dairy sour cream
1 teaspoon prepared mustard
1 teaspoon salt

1 Make corned-beef layer: Combine gelatin and sugar in a medium-size saucepan; stir in 1 cup of the water and bouillon cubes. Heat, stirring constantly, until gelatin and bouillon cubes dissolve. Remove from heat; stir in remaining 2 cups water and vinegar to mix well.
2 Measure ¾ cup into a small bowl; let stand at room temperature for Step 4. Pour remaining gelatin mixture into a large bowl; chill 30 minutes, or until as thick as unbeaten egg white.

3 Mash canned corned beef lightly with a fork, then stir into thickened gelatin with celery, green pepper and horseradish. Spoon into a 10-cup ring mold; chill just until sticky-firm.
4 While corned-beef layer chills, make potato-salad layer: Combine potatoes, cabbage, onion and parsley in a large bowl. Blend mayonnaise or salad dressing, sour cream, mustard and salt into the ¾ cup gelatin from Step 2; fold into potato mixture.
5 Spoon over sticky-firm corned-beef layer in mold; chill at least 4 hours, or until firm.
6 Just before serving, run a sharp-tip, thin-blade knife around top of mold, then dip mold *very quickly* in and out of a pan of hot water. Invert onto serving plate; carefully lift off mold. Garnish plate with salad greens and serve with additional mayonnaise or salad dressing, if you wish.

●

Redcap Veal Mousse
Tomato-aspic layer atop creamy-light veal salad makes this most inviting main dish.
Makes 6 to 8 servings

Tomato-Aspic Layer
1 envelope unflavored gelatin
1 cup water
1 can (8 ounces) tomato sauce
1 teaspoon lemon juice

Veal Layer
1 envelope unflavored gelatin
1 cup water
1 can (10½ ounces) condensed cream of celery soup
¼ cup mayonnaise or salad dressing
2 cups chopped cooked veal
¼ cup chopped toasted almonds (from a 5-ounce can)
1 tablespoon chopped parsley
1 teaspoon chopped chives

1 Make tomato-aspic layer: Soften gelatin in water in a small saucepan; heat, stirring constantly, just until gelatin dissolves; remove from heat.
2 Blend in tomato sauce and lemon juice; pour into an 8-cup mold; chill just until sticky-firm.
3 While tomato-aspic layer chills, make veal layer: Soften gelatin in water in a medium-size saucepan; heat, stirring constantly, just until gelatin dissolves. Stir in soup until mixture is smooth; remove from heat.
4 Blend in mayonnaise or salad dressing, then stir in veal, almonds, parsley and chives. Chill until as thick as unbeaten egg white.
5 Spoon over tomato-aspic layer in mold; chill several hours, or until firm.
6 Just before serving, run a sharp-tip, thin-

1376

blade knife around top of mold, then dip mold *very quickly* in and out of a pan of hot water. Invert onto serving plate; carefully lift off mold. Garnish with lemon wedges, and serve with additional mayonnaise or salad dressing, if you wish.

Shepherd's Pie

Flakes of golden carrots whipped into potatoes make its fluffy topper.
Bake at 375° for 30 minutes. Makes 4 to 6 servings

- 4 medium-size potatoes, pared and quartered
- 3 medium-size carrots, pared and quartered
- 2 packages (10 ounces each) frozen Fordhook limas
- 2 to 3 cups cubed cooked beef, veal or lamb roast or pot roast
- 1 can (about 11 ounces) beef gravy
- ½ cup milk
- 2 tablespoons butter or margarine
- 1 tablespoon minced onion

1 Cook potatoes and carrots together in boiling salted water in medium-size saucepan 20 minutes, or until tender; drain; mash. Cook lima beans in separate saucepan, following label directions; drain.

2 Combine meat cubes and lima beans in shallow 6-cup casserole; pour gravy over. (If using canned gravy, blend in ¾ cup water to make 2 cups.)

3 Heat milk, butter or margarine and onion in small saucepan; pour over mashed potatoes and carrots; beat until fluffy. Spoon in small mounds around edge of casserole; pile any remaining in middle.

4 Bake in moderate oven (375°) 30 minutes, or until bubbly-hot and potato trim is tipped with brown.

Beef or Veal Strips in Sour Cream

Just heat leftover meat in a no-fuss creamy sauce for this dinner treat.
Makes 4 to 6 servings

- 1 large onion, chopped (1 cup)
- 2 tablespoons butter or margarine
- 2 to 3 cups julienne strips of cooked beef or veal roast or pot roast
- 1 can (about 11 ounces) spaghetti sauce with mushrooms
- 1 cup dairy sour cream
  Buttered hot noodles

1 Sauté onion in butter or margarine in large frying pan; add meat and brown lightly.

Shepherd's Pie is hardly peasant fare—it's loaded with meat, carrots and limas and topped with potatoes.

Quick Ragout accommodatingly uses up leftover beef, veal or lamb roast with equal success.

1378

2 Stir in spaghetti sauce; simmer 5 minutes.
3 Stir in sour cream; heat *just to boiling.* Serve over buttered hot noodles.

Popover Ragout
Makes 4 servings

12 *small white onions, peeled (about ½ pound)*
 ¼ *pound green beans, tipped and cut into bite-size pieces (1 cup)*
 2 *large carrots, pared and cut into 1-inch pieces*
 ¾ *cup water*
 3 *tablespoons butter or margarine*
 3 *tablespoons all-purpose flour*
 ½ *teaspoon salt*
   Dash of pepper
 2 *teaspoons meat-flavor paste*
 2 *cups cubed cooked beef, veal or lamb*
 4 POPOVER SHELLS *(recipe follows)*

1 Cook onions, beans and carrots in ¾ cup water in covered large saucepan 15 minutes, or until vegetables are tender.
2 Drain and measure cooking liquid; add enough water to make 2 cups; save for Step 3; save vegetables for Step 5.
3 Melt butter or margarine in same saucepan;

remove from heat; blend in flour, salt and pepper; slowly stir in reserved 2 cups liquid and meat-flavor paste.
4 Cook over low heat, stirring constantly, until sauce thickens and boils 1 minute.
5 Add meat and cooked vegetables; set aside while you mix POPOVER SHELLS.
6 While shells bake, reheat stew; spoon into hot POPOVER SHELLS; serve at once.

Popover Shells
Bake at 450° for 15 minutes. Makes 4 shells

 2 *eggs*
 ½ *cup milk*
 ½ *cup sifted all-purpose flour*
 ⅛ *teaspoon salt*

1 Heavily butter 4 shallow (2-cup size) baking dishes, ramekins or small frying pans.
2 Beat eggs until foamy with rotary beater in 1-quart measure or medium-size bowl; stir in milk.
3 Sift flour and salt into egg mixture; beat 1 minute, or until no lumps remain.
4 Pour batter into prepared dishes (place on cookie sheet or in shallow baking pan for easy handling).

5 Bake in very hot oven (450°) 15 minutes, or until shells are puffed, crisp and golden-brown.

Meat 'n' Taters
Bake at 400° for 1 hour and 15 minutes. Makes 6 servings

    6 medium-size baking potatoes
    4 tablespoons butter or margarine (½ stick)
    1 teaspoon salt
    ⅛ teaspoon pepper
    1 small onion, grated
    ¾ to 1 cup milk
    1 cup chopped cooked beef, veal or lamb
    1 can (about 11 ounces) beef gravy

1 Wash and dry potatoes.
2 Bake in hot oven (400°) 1 hour, or until tender; leave oven on.
3 Cut tops from hot baked potatoes; scoop out centers into medium-size bowl; reserve shells.
4 Mash centers; blend butter or margarine, salt, pepper, onion and enough milk to make potatoes light and fluffy; stir in chopped meat.
5 Pile mixture back into reserved shells.
6 Bake in hot oven (400°) 15 minutes, or until tops are brown.
7 Heat gravy; serve over baked stuffed potatoes.

Chop-Chop Suey
Makes 4 to 6 servings

    2 tablespoons butter or margarine
    1 large onion, chopped (1 cup)
    1 can (about 1 pound) chop-suey vegetables
    1 cup sliced celery
    ½ teaspoon salt
      Dash of pepper
    2 cups finely diced cooked beef, veal or lamb
    2 tablespoons cornstarch
    2 teaspoons sugar
    ¼ cup water
    1 tablespoon soy sauce
    4 to 5 cups hot cooked rice (2 cups raw)

1 Melt butter or margarine in large frying pan; add onion; sauté over low heat about 10 minutes, or until onion is tender.
2 Drain chop-suey vegetables; measure ¾ cup

liquid; add to sautéed onion; stir in chop-suey vegetables, celery, salt and pepper; bring to boiling; reduce heat; simmer 5 minutes; add meat.
3 Combine cornstarch and sugar in cup; blend in water and soy sauce to make a smooth paste; stir into meat mixture.
4 Heat, stirring constantly, until mixture thickens; simmer 5 minutes.
5 Pile hot cooked rice in ring around edge of serving dish; spoon hot chop suey in center; if desired, garnish with pimiento strips.

Quick Ragout
With cooked meat cubes as your starter, this crisp-weather dandy can be ready in minutes. Makes 4 to 6 servings

    2 cups cubed cooked beef, veal or lamb roast
      or pot roast
    2 tablespoons butter or margarine
    1 can (about 11 ounces) beef gravy
    1 can (about 1 pound) peas
    4 to 6 onions, peeled and halved
    2 white turnips, pared and quartered
    1½ teaspoons salt
    ½ teaspoon leaf thyme, crumbled
    ⅛ teaspoon pepper
    2 stalks of celery, sliced in 1-inch lengths
    2 tomatoes, cut in wedges
    1 teaspoon sugar

1 Brown meat in butter or margarine in large heavy frying pan; stir in gravy, and liquid from peas; heat to boiling.
2 Arrange onions and turnips around meat; sprinkle with salt, thyme and pepper. Cover; cook 10 minutes; add celery; cook 10 minutes longer, or just until vegetables are tender.
3 Stir in peas; arrange tomatoes on top; sprinkle with sugar. Cover; cook 5 minutes longer. Serve over buttered hot noodles, if you wish.

1379

LUXURIOUS LEFTOVERS

Monterrey Mix
An easy supper dish to fix—and what a zippy blend of flavors!
Makes 4 to 6 servings

1 large onion, chopped (1 cup)
2 tablespoons olive oil or vegetable oil
1 tablespoon chili powder
2 to 3 cups diced cooked beef, veal or lamb
1 can (1 pound) red kidney beans
1 cup diced celery
1 can (about 1 pound) tomatoes
1 teaspoon sugar
1 teaspoon salt
¼ teaspoon pepper
1 to 1½ cups leftover rice, mashed potatoes or pasta

1 Sauté onion in olive oil or salad oil until softened in large frying pan; stir in chili powder and cook 1 minute.
2 Stir in remaining ingredients; cover; simmer 30 minutes to blend flavors.
3 Serve over hot corn bread, rice or buttered, toasted, split hard rolls.

Potluck Pie
Bake at 425° for 15 to 20 minutes. Makes 8 servings

1 package piecrust mix
2 cups finely diced cooked beef, veal or lamb
1 can (about 1 pound) mixed vegetables, drained
½ cup catsup
1 small onion, chopped (¼ cup)
¼ teaspoon leaf thyme, crumbled
¼ teaspoon salt
Dash of pepper
2 teaspoons melted butter or margarine

1 Prepare pastry according to directions on package; roll ⅔ of pastry on lightly floured pastry cloth or board to fit over bottom and sides of baking pan, 11x7x1½; cut overhang flush with edge of pan with pastry wheel or sharp knife.
2 Roll out remaining pastry to rectangle, 10x6; with pastry wheel or sharp knife cut lengthwise in half, crosswise in quarters to make 8 pieces; save for Step 4.*
3 Combine meat, mixed vegetables, catsup, onion, thyme, salt and pepper in medium-size bowl; toss lightly.

4 Spoon meat mixture in medium-size bowl; toss lightly.
5 Spoon meat mixture in even layer into pastry-lined pan; arrange pastry squares on top; brush with melted butter or margarine.
6 Bake in hot oven (425°) 15 to 20 minutes, or until pastry is golden-brown and filling is bubbly-hot.
*If desired, make pie in 9-inch pie plate, cutting an 8-inch round of pastry for topping into 8 wedges.

Red Devil Barbecue
Makes 4 to 6 servings

1 tablespoon butter or margarine
1 large onion, chopped (1 cup)
½ clove of garlic, minced
2 cups (about 1-pound can) tomatoes
1 tablespoon brown sugar
1 teaspoon chili powder
1 teaspoon dry mustard
1 teaspoon salt
⅛ teaspoon pepper
2 teaspoons cider vinegar
2 whole cloves
1 bay leaf
1½ cups cubed cooked beef or lamb
1 package (8 ounces) noodles
2 tablespoons chopped parsley

1 Melt butter or margarine in large frying pan; add onion and garlic; sauté over low heat about 10 minutes, or until onion is tender.
2 Stir in tomatoes, brown sugar, chili powder, dry mustard, salt, pepper, vinegar, whole cloves and bay leaf; heat to boiling; reduce heat; simmer 45 minutes, or until flavors are blended and mixture is about as thick as chili sauce.
3 Add meat cubes; simmer 10 to 15 minutes longer, or until meat is heated through.
4 While barbecue mixture simmers, cook noodles in large amount of boiling salted water until tender; drain; stir in chopped parsley.
5 Arrange parsley noodles in 2 rows on platter; spoon barbecued meat in rows.

1380

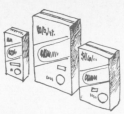

Pancake Bake

Layer jumbo corn cakes with a zippy beef filling for this Mexican-style casserole.
Bake at 400° for 30 minutes. Makes 6 servings

Filling

1 large onion, chopped (1 cup)
1 clove of garlic, minced
2 teaspoons chili powder
2 tablespoons olive oil or vegetable oil
2 cups crumbled leftover meat loaf
1 can (about 1 pound, 13 ounces) tomatoes
2 cans (about 1 pound each) red kidney beans
2 teaspoons sugar
2 teaspoons salt

Pancakes

1 egg
1 cup sifted all-purpose flour
½ cup yellow cornmeal
¼ teaspoon salt
1½ cups water

Topping

1 small onion, peeled, sliced and separated into rings
½ cup pitted ripe olives, sliced
1 cup grated Cheddar cheese (4 ounces)

1 Make filling: Sauté onion and garlic with chili powder in olive oil or vegetable oil just until soft in a large frying pan; stir in crumbled meat loaf, then remaining filling ingredients; cover. Simmer 15 minutes to blend flavors.
2 While sauce simmers, make pancakes: Beat egg until thick in a medium-size bowl; beat in flour, cornmeal, salt and water until smooth. (Batter will be thin.)
3 Heat a 9-inch heavy frying pan slowly; test temperature by sprinkling in a few drops of water. When drops bounce about, temperature is right; grease lightly. Pour batter, a scant ⅓ cup for each pancake, into pan; bake 3 minutes, or until top appears dry and underside is golden; turn; bake 2 minutes longer. Repeat to make 8 cakes.
4 As each is baked, layer with about 1 cup sauce between into a 12-cup baking dish, ending with pancake. (Pancakes take up sauce during baking.)
5 Arrange topping: Place onion rings and sliced olives in a pretty pattern on top; sprinkle with cheese.

6 Bake, uncovered, in hot oven (400°) 30 minutes, or until bubbly-hot. Cut into wedges.

Lamb-Stuffed Cabbage Leaves

Ground cooked lamb plus crisp bacon go into the savory filling to steam inside big green cabbage leaves.
Makes 6 servings, 3 rolls each

1 large head of cabbage
4 cups ground cooked lamb
8 slices crisp bacon, crumbled
¾ cup soda cracker crumbs (about 16)
1 medium-size onion, chopped (½ cup)
1 small clove of garlic, minced
1 cup tomato juice
2 eggs, slightly beaten
½ teaspoon salt
⅛ teaspoon pepper
3 tablespoons butter or margarine
1 vegetable-bouillon cube
1 cup hot water (for rolls)
1 tablespoon all-purpose flour
1 tablespoon water (for gravy)

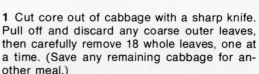

1 Cut core out of cabbage with a sharp knife. Pull off and discard any coarse outer leaves, then carefully remove 18 whole leaves, one at a time. (Save any remaining cabbage for another meal.)
2 Steam leaves, covered, in a small amount of boiling salted water in a large frying pan 8 minutes, or just until limp; drain well.
3 Combine lamb, bacon, cracker crumbs, onion, garlic, tomato juice, eggs, salt and pepper in a large bowl; mix lightly with a fork until blended.
4 Lay cabbage leaves flat; place 2 to 3 tablespoons meat mixture in middle of each. Fold thick end up over filling, then fold both sides toward middle. Roll up, jelly-roll fashion, to cover filling completely; fasten with one or two wooden picks.
5 Brown rolls, a few at a time, in butter or margarine in a large frying pan. Pile all rolls back into pan.
6 Dissolve bouillon cube in the 1 cup hot water in a 1-cup measure; pour over rolls; cover. Steam 20 minutes, or until cabbage is tender. Remove to a heated serving platter; keep hot while making gravy.

1381

7 Pour drippings from pan into a 1-cup measure; add water, if needed, to make 1 cup; return to pan. Blend flour with the 1 tablespoon water until smooth in a cup; stir into liquid in pan. Cook over low heat, stirring constantly, until gravy thickens and boils 1 minute. Season to taste with salt and pepper. Pour into a heated bowl to spoon over cabbage rolls.

Cumberland Lamb Pie
Cubed cooked lamb plus leftover gravy are turned into a second-day best.
Bake at 400° for 35 minutes. Makes 6 servings

1 medium-size onion, chopped (½ cup)
1 clove of garlic, minced
¼ pound fresh mushrooms, chopped
2 tablespoons butter or margarine
2 cups canned beef gravy (from 2 about-11-ounce cans)
½ cup water
Dash of ground cloves
5 cups cubed cooked lamb
1 can (1 pound) small whole carrots, drained
Pastry for one 9-inch single-crust pie

1 Sauté onion, garlic and mushrooms in butter or margarine in a large frying pan 5 minutes, or until onion is soft. Add gravy, water and cloves, stirring to mix well; heat to boiling.
2 Place lamb and carrots in an 8-cup shallow baking dish; pour gravy mixture over. Keep hot.
3 Make pastry with piecrust mix, following label directions, or use your favorite recipe. Roll out on a lightly floured pastry cloth or board to a circle or rectangle 1 inch larger than baking dish; cut several slits in middle to let steam escape; cover pie. Trim overhang to ½ inch; turn under, flush with rim; press all around with a fork to seal.
4 Bake in hot oven (400°) 35 minutes, or until pastry is golden and gravy bubbles up. To serve, cut pastry into wedges or blocks, then spoon out the filling.

1382

Scotch Broth
After most of your roast disappears, simmer flavor from bones for this old-time soup.
Makes 8 servings

Bones from lamb roast
8 cups water
2 large onions, chopped (2 cups)
½ cup pearl barley
3 teaspoons salt
⅛ teaspoon pepper
6 medium-size carrots, pared and finely diced (2 cups)
2 tablespoons chopped parsley

1 Combine lamb bones with water and half of the onion in a large kettle. (Save remaining onion for Step 3.) Cover; heat to boiling, then simmer 2 to 3 hours, or until all meat falls off bones.
2 Strain broth into a large saucepan; cool, then chill until fat rises to top; skim off. Measure broth, adding water, if needed, to make 8 cups; return to kettle.
3 Stir in remaining onion, barley, salt and pepper; cover. Simmer 40 minutes; stir in carrots. Continue cooking 20 minutes, or until carrots are tender.
4 Ladle into heated soup bowls; sprinkle with parsley.

Monday Croquettes
Makes 4 servings, 2 patties each

3 tablespoons butter or margarine
3 tablespoons all-purpose flour
½ teaspoon salt
⅛ teaspoon pepper
1 cup milk
2 cups cooked rice
1 cup finely chopped cooked beef or lamb
1 medium-size onion, finely chopped
2 tablespoons chopped parsley
1 egg, slightly beaten

1 Melt butter or margarine in medium-size saucepan; remove from heat; blend in flour, salt and pepper; slowly stir in milk.
2 Cook over low heat, stirring constantly, until sauce thickens and boils 1 minute; remove from heat.
3 Combine rice, meat, onion, parsley and egg in large bowl; blend in sauce; chill several hours, or until mixture is firm enough to handle.
4 Shape mixture into 8 patties, about 2½ inches in diameter.
5 Sauté in small amount of hot vegetable shortening in large frying pan over medium heat 10 to 15 minutes, or until brown; turn and brown second side. If desired, serve with chili sauce.

Lamb 'n' Potato Cakes
Bits and pieces make these hearty patties.
Makes 4 servings

1 medium-size onion, finely chopped (½ cup)
  Bacon drippings
2 cups finely chopped cold cooked lamb
3 medium-size potatoes, cooked, peeled and
  finely chopped
1 egg
1 tablespoon catsup
1 tablespoon bottled gravy coloring

1 Sauté onion in 1 tablespoon drippings in large
frying pan 2 to 3 minutes, or just until softened.
2 Stir in lamb, potatoes, egg and catsup. Season with salt and pepper, if needed. Mix well.
3 Shape into 8 even-size patties; brush each
lightly on both sides with gravy coloring.
4 Sauté in same frying pan, adding more drippings as needed, until heated through and well
browned.

Farm-Style Lamb Stew
Makes 8 servings

4 cups cubed cooked lamb
4 tablespoons (½ stick) butter or margarine

1 package (6 ounces) frozen whole
  mushrooms
2 packages (10 ounces each) frozen mixed
  vegetables in butter sauce
1 package (8 ounces) frozen onions in cream
  sauce
1 envelope onion-sauce mix
2 cups water
1½ cups biscuit mix
1 teaspoon mixed salad herbs
½ cup milk

1 Brown lamb in butter or margarine in a Dutch
oven; stir in frozen mushrooms; sauté 2 minutes.
2 Remove frozen mixed vegetables from cooking bag and add to meat mixture with frozen
onions, onion-sauce mix and water; heat to
boiling; separating vegetables with a fork as
they thaw; cover. Simmer 15 minutes.
3 While vegetables cook, combine biscuit mix
and herbs in a medium-size bowl; add milk all
at once; stir lightly just until flour is moistened.
Drop in 8 mounds on top of bubbling stew.
4 Cook, uncovered, 10 minutes; cover. Cook
10 minutes longer, or until dumplings are
fluffy-light.

1383

**MOVABLE FEASTS:
PICNIC GROUND GRILL-ABLES,
COOK-IN CARRY-OUTS, SALAD
PACKABLES, SWEETS TO PACK UP
AND GO, STURDY COOKIE
TRAVELERS**

Picnicking today isn't just a matter of packing up a basket of sandwiches, another of crispy fried chicken, a jug of lemonade or iced tea and heading for the old millstream.

First of all, the old millstream probably no longer exists and, if it does, it more than likely isn't the choice picnic spot it once was. Most picnics now take place in the city, county, state and federal parks and picnic grounds that are popping up all over the country. Because these come equipped with tables (many of them inside shelters), with grills and, in some instances, with running water, picnic menus have changed dramatically.

There is no reason today why a giant steak or side of spareribs can't be carted to the picnic ground and grilled or barbecued there. Or why a gallon or so of stew or a whopping casserole can't be made at home, transferred to the picnic ground and heated up there.

The paraphernalia of picnicking has proliferated along with the appearance of picnic grounds so that any gourmet feast can be safely and successfully transported. Frozen foods will stay frozen, chilled foods chilled, hot foods hot. Moreover, supermarkets are well stocked with paper plates, cups and napkins as well as with mini-plastic packs of salt and pepper, mustard, ketchup, even soy and Chinese plum sauce.

Picnics today are truly al fresco feasts, often with a foreign flavor because serving away from home need not be any more difficult than dishing up food in your own backyard. In the pages that follow, you'll find a collection of frankly unpicniclike recipes that you can cook (or at least partially prepare) in your own kitchen *and* take with you. There are packing tips to tell you how.

Steak on a picnic? Easily done if there's a grill at the picnic ground. Party Steak Diane is the name of this one. Also shown, portable Duxbury Burgers.

PICNIC GROUND GRILL-ABLES

Party Steak Diane
Makes 8 to 10 servings

- 1 sirloin steak, cut 2 inches thick and weighing 5 pounds
- 1 teaspoon freshly ground pepper
- ½ cup (1 stick) butter or margarine
- 2 teaspoons dry mustard
- ¾ pound fresh mushrooms, washed, trimmed and sliced
- 1½ cups sliced green onions

1 tablespoon lemon juice
1 tablespoon Worcestershire sauce
1 teaspoon salt
¼ cup chopped parsley

1 Remove steak from refrigerator 1 hour before cooking. Trim off any excess fat, then score remaining fat edge every inch so that meat will lie flat on grill. Sprinkle pepper over both sides; rub in well.
2 Melt butter or margarine in a medium-size frying pan on grill over hot coals; stir in mustard, mushrooms and onions. Sauté 10 minutes, or until onions are soft. Stir in lemon juice, Worcestershire sauce, salt and parsley; remove from heat.
3 When ready to cook meat, rub hot grill with a few fat trimmings to help prevent sticking. Place steak on grill about 6 inches above hot coals. Grill 15 minutes; brush lightly with part of butter mixture from sauce; grill 5 minutes longer. Turn steak; grill 20 minutes; brush lightly with sauce. Grill 5 minutes longer for rare, or until steak is as done as you like it. To test for doneness, cut a small slit near bone. Place steak on a cutting board; garnish with a tomato rose and parsley, if you wish.
4 Reheat remaining sauce; spoon part over steak. Slice steak ¼ inch thick; serve remaining sauce separately.
Note—Prepare everything on the picnic grill.

Duxbury Burgers
Makes 8 servings

1 package (8 ounces) ready-mix herb-seasoned stuffing
1¼ cups hot water
½ cup (1 stick) butter or margarine, melted
2 eggs, lightly beaten
3 pounds ground beef
Salt
1 can (8 ounces) whole cranberry sauce
2 tablespoons vegetable oil
1 tablespoon prepared mustard
1 can (about 11 ounces) beef gravy
8 hero rolls, split

1 Combine stuffing mix, hot water and melted butter or margarine in a large bowl; toss until evenly moist. Stir in eggs; cool completely.
2 Divide ground beef into 8 parts. Shape each into a 4-inch square, then roll between sheets of wax paper to an 8-inch square. (Tip: To prevent slipping, lay paper on top of damp paper toweling.) Sprinkle meat lightly with salt.

1386

3 Spread about ⅓ cup of the cooled stuffing mixture over each square; roll up, jelly-roll fashion. Place in a single layer on a cookie sheet; cover. Chill until cooking time.
4 Combine cranberry sauce, vegetable oil and mustard in an electric-blender container; cover; beat until smooth. (If you do not have a blender, beat ingredients at high speed with an electric beater.)
5 When ready to cook meat, place on grill about 6 inches above hot coals. Grill 10 minutes; turn. Cook 10 minutes longer; brush with part of the cranberry mixture. Continue cooking, turning and brushing often, 5 minutes, or until meat is richly glazed and as done as you like it.
6 While meat cooks, heat gravy in a small saucepan and warm rolls on grill.
7 Place each burger in a roll; garnish with small onion rings, if you wish. Serve gravy separately.
Note—Stuff and shape meat and fix cranberry mixture at home; carry to your eating spot in a keep-cold container.

Stuffed Chicken Roma
Makes 6 servings

6 chicken breasts, weighing about 12 ounces each
2 tablespoons finely chopped green onion
½ cup (1 stick) butter or margarine
1½ cups fresh bread crumbs
¼ pound soft salami, finely chopped

1 Bone chicken breasts, leaving skin in place. Place flat, skin side down, on a cutting board.
2 Sauté onion in 3 tablespoons of the butter or margarine until soft in a small frying pan; stir in bread crumbs and salami until evenly moist.
3 Divide stuffing into 6 parts; spoon along hollows in chicken breasts. Fold edges of chicken over stuffing to cover completely; fasten with wooden picks.
4 Melt remaining butter or margarine in a small saucepan on grill; brush part over chicken. Place breasts on grill, buttered side down, about 6 inches above hot coals. Grill 20 minutes. Brush again with melted butter or margarine; turn. Grill 20 minutes longer, or until chicken is tender and golden. Place on a large serving platter; remove picks. Garnish with carrot curls and sprigs of chicory, if you wish.
Note—If traveling a distance to your eating spot, make stuffing and chill well, then stuff into chicken breasts and keep chilled until cooking time.

Dunkin' Ribs
Makes 4 servings

3½ pounds country-style spareribs
Salt
Pepper
SOY DIP *(recipe follows)*

1 Trim any excess fat from ribs; cut ribs apart, if needed. Season with salt and pepper.
2 Rub hot grill with a few fat trimmings to help prevent sticking. Place ribs on grill about 8 inches above hot coals.
3 Grill slowly, turning often, 1½ hours, or until meat is tender. Place ribs on a large serving platter; serve hot with SOY DIP.

   SOY DIP—Mix 1 tablespoon cornstarch with ¼ cup water until smooth in a small saucepan; stir in ½ cup peach preserves, ¼ cup soy sauce and 1 teaspoon salt. Cook, stirring constantly, until mixture thickens and boils 3 minutes. Remove from heat; stir in 2 tablespoons dry sherry. Serve warm. Makes about 1 cup.
Note—Make dip at home and carry to your eating spot in a jar with a tight lid, then reheat on edge of grill while ribs cook.

Double Sausage Winders
Makes 8 servings

2 medium-size tomatoes, finely chopped
1 medium-size onion, finely chopped (½ cup)
3 tablespoons finely chopped celery
2 tablespoons finely chopped sweet red pepper
1 tablespoon cider vinegar
¾ teaspoon salt
⅛ teaspoon pepper
8 frankfurters
4 heat-and-serve sausage links
8 slices bacon, partly cooked
8 frankfurter rolls
4 tablespoons (½ stick) butter or margarine
1 teaspoon leaf thyme, crumbled

1 Mix tomatoes, onion, celery, red pepper, vinegar, salt and pepper in a small bowl. Chill several hours or overnight to season.
2 Slit each frankfurter lengthwise almost to bottom; quarter sausages lengthwise. Stuff 2 quarters into each frankfurter; wrap a slice of partly cooked bacon around each; fasten with dampened wooden picks.
3 Place on grill about 6 inches above hot coals. Grill, turning several times, 8 minutes, or until bacon is crisp and frankfurters are heated through.

4 While meat cooks, toast rolls on side of grill. Melt butter or margarine in a small saucepan on grill; stir in thyme; brush over cut side of rolls.
5 Serve each frankfurter in a roll; top with the tomato relish.
Note—Stuff frankfurters and wrap with bacon ahead, then carry, ready to grill, to your eating spot. Take along tomato relish in a tightly covered jar.

PICNIC-GROUND CHEFS—
THESE COOKING TIPS ARE FOR YOU:

No fancy gear needed. Just a sunny day and a hungry crowd, and you're set for the most fun-in-the-world way of cooking. The easy hints here will help new outdoor chefs to build their first fire right and old hands to enjoy the job even more.

Starting Point: The Fire
Getting the fire going is the same, whether your grill is a rack propped up on two stones or a fancy store-brought model. Unless you live where slow-burning woods such as hickory, oak, maple, walnut and olive are abundant, buy charcoal briquettes, sold by the bag in varying weights. They start fast, burn slowly without spitting out sparks, and give an intense heat. Knowing how much charcoal to use is also important, as a fire that's too small slows down cooking and one that's too big simply wastes fuel. A good rule of thumb: You'll need more charcoal for thick steaks or other cuts of meat that take a long time to cook than for hot dogs or hamburgers or other quick-grill choices.

Lighting the Fire
For easy starting, buy one of the many packaged starter fuels on the market. Choices are many—liquid, jelly, a combination box of charcoal and lighter, even an electric lighter to plug into an outdoor outlet. Be sure to read label directions, and for complete safety, follow them to the letter. Another tip: Before starting any fire, know how to put it out—fast! Sand is your best helper.

Be Patient
A single layer of briquettes will take a minimum of 30 minutes to heat through; a deep fire bed, longer. Briquettes are ready when they turn ash-gray. At night, you can also detect a red glow, but the ash-gray look is your best guide. They hold their heat for a long time, so you needn't be in a rush to start cooking. Budget note: If fire bed is still active when you finish

1387

cooking, pick out the briquettes with tongs, dunk in water, and dry, ready to use again.

"First Aid" for Too-Hot, Too-Cool Fire

Know-how is simple for these problems. If the fire is too hot, just lower the firebox or raise the grill, if they're adjustable. Or move the food to the edge of the grill, away from intense heat. Fire too cool? Tap the ash off the briquettes, it's an insulator, and if possible, lower the grill, nearer to the heat. Better still, wait awhile before loading the grill with food.

What about Tools?

You can do nicely with a few carefully chosen ones, or go all out—even to a chef's hat. Whatever your choice, buy good-quality utensils, as they will reward you in long service. A few musts: A long-handle fork plus heavy tongs for turning big steaks or thick cuts of meat . . . a long-handle spoon for stirring . . . a two-inch quality paintbrush and heavy saucepan with flat bottom and heatproof handle for sauce spreader and container. Others that will be a big help are large, easy-grasp salt and pepper shakers; roll of heavy foil for all kinds of jobs from lining firebox (foil reflects heat faster) to making disposable pans for heating rolls and vegetables, or keeping foods hot for second helpings; asbestos pot holders or mitts.

Over-the-Coals Tricks with Meat

Trim fat edges of steaks, ham and chops to prevent drippings from falling into the fire and blazing up. Score edge of meat to keep it from ruffling up during cooking, or grill in a wire broiler basket.

COOK-IN CARRY-OUTS

1388

Kettle Veal Dinner
Makes 6 servings

    2 pounds boneless veal shoulder
    2 tablespoons butter or margarine
 2½ cups water
    2 teaspoons salt
    1 teaspoon leaf thyme, crumbled
    1 bay leaf
    ¼ teaspoon pepper
    1 envelope instant chicken broth
       OR: 1 teaspoon granulated chicken bouillon
    1 can (1 pound) whole boiled onions, drained
    1 package (10 ounces) frozen peas
    1 can (3 or 4 ounces) sliced mushrooms

    ¼ cup flour
    1 small loaf French bread, sliced

1 Trim any fat from veal; cut meat into 1-inch cubes. Brown in butter or margarine in a heavy kettle or Dutch oven.
2 Stir in 2 cups of the water, salt, thyme, bay leaf, pepper and chicken broth. Heat to boiling; cover.
3 Simmer 1 hour and 15 minutes, or until veal is almost tender; remove bay leaf: Stir in onions, frozen peas and mushrooms and liquid; cover again. Cook 15 minutes, or until peas and veal are tender.
4 Mix flour with remaining ½ cup water until smooth in a cup; stir into veal mixture. Cook, stirring constantly, until mixture thickens and boils 1 minute.
5 Ladle over slices of French bread in soup plates.
Note—Chill stew if made ahead; reheat in kettle on a grill at picnic spot. Be sure kettle has heatproof handles.

Stefado
Makes 8 servings

 1½ pounds boneless beef chuck
    1 pound boneless lamb shoulder
    2 tablespoons vegetable oil
    1 medium-size onion, chopped (½ cup)
    3 teaspoons salt
    1 teaspoon leaf marjoram
    ¼ teaspoon ground allspice
    ¼ teaspoon pepper
    1 bay leaf
    4 cups water
    2 cans (1 pound each) stewed tomatoes
    1 small eggplant, weighing about 1 pound, trimmed and diced
    1 package (8 ounces) elbow macaroni
    ¼ cup chopped parsley

1 Trim fat from beef and lamb; cut meats into 1-inch cubes, keeping them separate.
2 Brown lamb in 1 tablespoon of the vegetable oil in a heavy kettle or Dutch oven; remove with a slotted spoon to a pan.
3 Brown beef in remaining 1 tablespoon vegetable oil in same kettle; push to one side. Add onion and sauté 2 minutes. Stir in 2 teaspoons of the salt, marjoram, allspice, pepper, bay leaf and 2 cups of the water. Heat to boiling; cover.
4 Simmer, stirring several times, 1 hour. Stir in lamb; cover. Simmer 30 minutes, or until meats are almost tender. Stir in tomatoes and egg-

plant; cover. Simmer 30 minutes, or until meats are tender.

5 Stir in remaining 1 teaspoon salt and 2 cups water; heat to boiling; slowly stir in macaroni. Cook, stirring several times, 10 minutes, or until macaroni is tender. Remove bay leaf. Sprinkle with parsley.

6 Ladle into soup bowls. Serve with crusty bread, if you wish.

Note—Chill stew if made ahead, then reheat on grill at your eating spot in a kettle with heatproof handles. If stew seems too thick, stir in about ½ cup water.

Bratwurst Bake
Bake at 350° for 45 minutes. Makes 6 servings

　6 *fully cooked bratwurst*
　1 *tablespoon vegetable oil*
　1 *large onion, peeled and sliced*
　1 *clove of garlic, minced*
　1 *can (1 pound) Italian tomatoes*
　1 *can (6 ounces) tomato paste*
　1 *tablespoon leaf oregano, crumbled*
1½ *teaspoons salt*
　¼ *teaspoon pepper*
　1 *tablespoon bottled steak sauce*
　2 *cans (1 pound, 4 ounces each) chick peas, drained*

1 Brown bratwurst in vegetable oil in a Dutch oven; remove from pan with a slotted spoon.
2 Add onion and garlic to drippings in Dutch oven; sauté until soft.
3 Stir in tomatoes and paste, oregano, salt, pepper, steak sauce and chick peas. Heat 3 minutes, or until bubbly. Arrange bratwurst on top. Do not cover.
4 Bake in moderate oven (350°) 45 minutes, or until bubbly.

Note—Chill if made ahead, then reheat on grill at your eating spot.

Seafood Slumgullion
Makes 6 servings

3 *large potatoes, pared and sliced thin (3 cups)*
1 *large onion, chopped (1 cup)*
1 *large green pepper, halved, seeded and cubed*
½ *cup (1 stick) butter or margarine*
2 *teaspoons salt*
1 *teaspoon leaf thyme, crumbled*
¼ *teaspoon pepper*
1 *can (16 ounces) tomato-clam cocktail*

1 *package (1 pound) frozen cod, partly thawed*
1 *package (1 pound) frozen deveined shelled raw shrimps*
2 *tablespoons minced parsley*

1 Sauté potatoes, onion, and green pepper in butter or margarine until soft in a heavy kettle or Dutch oven.
2 Stir in salt, thyme, pepper and tomato-clam cocktail; heat to boiling.
3 Cut cod into 1-inch chunks; add to kettle; cover. Simmer 10 minutes. Stir in shrimps; cook 10 minutes longer, or until shrimps are tender and cod flakes easily. Stir in parsley.
4 Ladle into soup bowls.

Note—Chill mixture if made ahead, then reheat on grill at your picnic spot in a kettle with heat-proof handles.

Campground Cassoulet
Bake at 400° for 1 hour. Makes 8 generous servings

4 *slices bacon, diced*
2 *pounds lean boneless lamb shoulder, cut into 1-inch cubes*
1 *large onion, chopped (1 cup)*
1 *sweet Italian sausage, sliced ¼-inch thick*
2 *cans (about 1 pound each) white kidney beans*
1 *can (about 1 pound) stewed tomatoes*
1 *teaspoon salt*
¼ *teaspoon pepper*
1 *bay leaf*

1 Cook bacon until crisp in a large frying pan; remove and place in a 10-cup flameproof bean pot or deep baking dish.
2 Brown lamb slowly, about half at a time, in bacon drippings; drain off all fat. Return all meat to pan; cover. Cook slowly 15 minutes. Remove with slotted spoon and place in bean pot with bacon.
3 Sauté onion just until soft in same frying pan; stir in sausage and sauté about 5 minutes. Add beans and liquid, tomatoes, salt, pepper and bay leaf; heat to boiling. Stir into meat mixture.
4 Bake, covered, in hot oven (400°) 30 minutes; uncover. Bake 30 minutes longer, or until lamb is tender. Remove bay leaf.

Note—Cover bean pot, then wrap in a double thickness of heavy foil and reheat on grill at your picnic spot.

1389

Beef Pielets

Seasoned ground beef bakes inside a rich pastry jacket to make this picnic-best finger food.

Bake at 400° for 20 minutes. Makes 8 pielets

1 pound ground beef
1 small onion, grated
1 egg
½ cup soft bread crumbs (1 slice)
1 tablespoon catsup
½ teaspoon Worcestershire sauce
1 teaspoon salt
⅛ teaspoon pepper
1 package piecrust mix

1 Combine ground beef and onion in a medium-size bowl; shape into large patty in a medium-size frying pan. Brown 5 minutes on each side, then break up into small chunks with a fork.
2 Beat egg slightly in a small bowl; stir in bread crumbs, catsup. Worcestershire sauce, salt and pepper. Drizzle over meat.
3 Cook, stirring constantly, about a minute; cool while making pastry.
4 Prepare piecrust mix, following label directions. Roll out half to a 12-inch square on lightly floured pastry cloth or board; cut into 4 six-inch squares with pastry wheel or knife.
5 Spoon about ¼ cup meat mixture onto center of each; fold over to make a triangle. Press edges firmly with a fork to seal, then trim off any thin edges to make straight and even. Place pielets on ungreased cookie sheet. Repeat with remaining half of pastry and meat mixture to make 8 pielets.
6 Bake in hot oven (400°) 20 minutes, or until pastry is golden. Remove from cookie sheet; cool on wire racks. Pielets taste best if served at room temperature rather than being chilled.
Note—Wrap each cooled pielet separately in wax paper, foil or transparent wrap, then pack in a box or basket.

SALAD PACKABLES

Summer Garden Potato Salad

Most popular of all picnic salads—this one with an easy molding trick.
Makes 6 servings

6 large potatoes, cooked, peeled and cut into small cubes
3 hard-cooked eggs, shelled and chopped

¾ cup chopped dill pickles
¾ cup sliced radishes
½ cup chopped green onions
1 teaspoon salt
1 teaspoon dillweed
¼ teaspoon pepper
1¼ cups mayonnaise
Salad greens
STUFFED-EGG DAISIES (recipe follows)
Cherry tomatoes

1 Combine potatoes, eggs, pickles, radishes, green onions, salt, dillweed and pepper in large bowl; stir in mayonnaise, mixing with a spoon until thoroughly blended (mixture will be moist). Chill at least 2 hours to blend and mellow flavors.
2 When ready to put salad together, break salad greens into bite-size pieces in large salad bowl; mound potato salad into a cone on top (it will pat quickly into shape with 2 spoons). Surround cone with STUFFED-EGG DAISIES and cherry tomatoes.
Note—Cover lightly with transparent wrap or foil. Or set bowl in shallow box and pack crumpled paper around it to hold it steady. Keep cool en route in an insulated tote bag or foam chest.

Stuffed-Egg Daisies

Each perky flower-shape cup hides a tangy stuffed olive.

Hard-cook and shell 6 eggs. Holding each upright, draw a guideline around middle with tip of knife, then make even saw-tooth cuts into egg above and below the line all the way around. Carefully pull halves apart; remove yolks and mash in small bowl. Blend in 2 tablespoons mayonnaise, 1 teaspoon prepared mustard and salt and pepper to taste. Place a small stuffed green olive in each egg-white half, then fill with yolk mixture; chill. Makes 6 servings.
Note—Pack in refrigerator egg-storage pan or throwaway foil pie or cake pan; cover lightly with transparent wrap or foil and carry to picnic ground in insulated cooler.

Twin-Bean Salad

Red kidney beans, green limas and crisp vegetables take on the snap of a zippy French dressing.
Makes 6 servings

2 packages (10 ounces each) frozen lima beans

2 *tablespoons grated onion*
MUSTARD DRESSING *(recipe follows)*
2 *cans (about 1 pound each) red kidney beans, drained*
½ *cup chopped celery*
1 *teaspoon garlic salt*
1 *teaspoon Worcestershire sauce*
1 *head of lettuce, shredded*
1 *can (9 ounces) ripe olives, drained*
1 *cup thinly sliced raw carrots*

1 Cook lima beans in large saucepan, following label directions; drain; place in medium-size bowl. Stir in onion and ¼ cup MUSTARD DRESSING; cover; chill.
2 Place drained kidney beans in second medium-size bowl. Stir in celery, garlic salt, Worcestershire sauce and ¼ cup MUSTARD DRESSING; cover; chill.
3 When ready to put salad together, place shredded lettuce in an insulated bucket. Spoon lima-bean and kidney-bean salads in 2 piles on top and separate with a row of olives. Edge lima beans with carrot slices; serve with remaining dressing.
MUSTARD DRESSING—Combine ¾ cup vegetable oil, ⅓ cup vinegar, 1 tablespoon prepared mustard and 1 teaspoon salt in small jar with tight-fitting cover. Shake to blend well. Makes about 1 cup.
Note—Carry and keep salad covered in insulated bucket until ready to serve.

Picnic Chef's Salad
It travels beautifully with all the makings packed separately.
Makes 8 servings

1 *head of leaf or Boston lettuce*
1 *head of romaine*
1 *bunch of watercress*
1 *bunch of green onions*
1 *bunch of radishes*
½ *pound sliced corned beef, cut in thin strips*
½ *pound sliced process American cheese, cut in thin strips*
½ *pound sliced process Swiss cheese, cut in thin strips*
4 *hard-cooked eggs, shelled and quartered*
1 *cucumber, sliced*
1 *bottle (10 ounces) stuffed green olives, drained*
1 *package (about 4 ounces) croutons*
  Vegetable oil
  Cider vinegar
  Salt and pepper

1 Wash and drain salad greens well; wash and trim onions and radishes. Wrap separately in

transparent wrap or foil, or pack in plastic bags; chill until picnic time.
2 Line 2 baskets or deep trays with transparent wrap; arrange greens and onions in one; place meat, cheeses, eggs, cucumber, radishes and olives in separate mounds in another; cover both lightly to keep foods moist. Leave croutons right in their own package.
3 At serving time, set out all the makings with salad bowls for each to make his own salad.
Note—Tote covered baskets or set trays in picnic cooler chest or sturdy cardboard box. Pack bottles of oil and vinegar, package of croutons and salt and pepper shakers in small box.

Picnic Potato Cones
Makes 8 servings

6 *medium-size potatoes, pared and diced*
1½ *cups dairy sour cream*
1 *envelope blue-cheese salad dressing mix*
1 *cup finely chopped celery*
2 *packages (6 ounces each) sliced ham-bologna (16 slices)*
  Parsley

1 Cook potatoes, covered, in boiling salted water in a large saucepan 15 minutes, or until tender; drain. Return potatoes to pan and shake over low heat until dry and fluffy. Press through a ricer or mash in a large bowl; cool slightly.
2 Blend sour cream and blue-cheese dressing mix in a small bowl; beat into potatoes; stir in celery.
3 Curl each slice of ham-bologna into a cornucopia; fasten with a wooden pick. Spoon potato mixture into each to fill. (Or press through a pastry bag into cornucopias.) Arrange in a single layer on a large serving platter; cover. Chill at least 2 hours to season.
4 Just before serving, garnish each cornucopia with a tiny sprig of parsley; garnish platter with lettuce and radish roses, if you wish.
Note—Wrap platter tightly and carry as is in an insulated cooler to your eating spot.

1391

Mustard Bean Bowl
Makes 6 servings

1 *can (1 pound, 4 ounces) white kidney beans, drained*
1 *can (1 pound) red kidney beans, drained*
1 *clove of garlic, crushed*
1 *package (10 ounces) fresh spinach*

½ cup mayonnaise or salad dressing
½ cup dairy sour cream
2 tablespoons prepared mustard
½ teaspoon seasoned salt
¼ teaspoon seasoned pepper

1 Place white and red beans in separate bowls; toss each with half of the garlic; cover. Let stand several hours to season.
2 Trim stems and any coarse leaves from spinach; wash leaves and dry well; break into bite-size pieces. Place in a large salad bowl; spoon beans in separate sections on top.
3 Blend mayonnaise or salad dressing with sour cream, mustard, salt and pepper in a small bowl; pour over bean mixture. Toss lightly to mix.
Note—Place beans and dressing in separate containers and spinach in a transparent bag, ready to put together at your eating spot.

Chicken Salad Mimosa
Makes 4 to 6 servings

   4 chicken breasts, weighing about 12 ounces each
1¾ teaspoons salt
   Few celery tops
   2 cups water
   1 cup chopped celery
   2 tablespoons chopped green onions
   2 tablespoons chopped pimiento
   1 bottle (8 ounces) coleslaw dressing
   3 tablespoons lemon juice
 ⅛ teaspoon pepper
   Romaine
   2 tablespoons toasted slivered almonds
   1 hard-cooked egg, shelled and cut up

1 Combine chicken breasts with ¼ teaspoon of the salt, celery tops and water in a large frying pan. Heat to boiling; cover. Simmer 30 minutes, or until chicken is tender. Remove from broth; cool until easy to handle, then pull off skin and take meat from bones; dice meat. Combine with celery, green onions and pimiento in a medium-size bowl.
2 Blend coleslaw dressing, lemon juice, remaining 1½ teaspoons salt and pepper in a small bowl. Pour over chicken mixture; toss lightly to mix. Chill at least 2 hours to season.
3 When ready to serve, line a large salad bowl with romaine. Add almonds to chicken mixture; toss lightly; spoon into bowl. Press hard-cooked egg through a sieve over top.
Note—Pack chicken salad, sieved egg and romaine separately; assemble at your eating spot.

1392

Polynesian Rice Salad
Makes 6 servings

 1 cup uncooked regular rice
¼ pound mushrooms
½ cup vegetable oil
¼ cup cider vinegar
 2 tablespoons soy sauce
½ teaspoon salt
 1 can (11 ounces) mandarin-orange segments, drained
 1 cup thinly sliced celery
 1 can (5 ounces) water chestnuts, drained and sliced
 2 tablespoons thinly sliced green onions
   Iceberg lettuce

1 Cook rice, following label directions; spoon into a large bowl.
2 While rice cooks, trim mushrooms, wash and dry well; slice lengthwise. Add to rice.
3 Combine vegetable oil, vinegar, soy sauce and salt in a jar with a tight lid; shake well to mix. Pour over rice mixture; toss lightly to mix; cover. Chill at least an hour to season.
4 Just before serving, fold in mandarin-orange segments; celery, water chestnuts and green onions. Spoon into a lettuce-lined bowl.
Note—Pack salad and lettuce separately; assemble at your eating spot.

Tomato Cups Provençale
Makes 6 servings

 6 medium-size potatoes, pared and diced
½ cup bottled oil-and-vinegar dressing
 6 large tomatoes
 2 hard-cooked eggs, shelled and diced
 1 can (2 ounces) anchovy fillets, drained and chopped
¼ cup sliced pitted ripe olives
 3 tablespoons chopped parsley
 1 tablespoon finely cut chives

1 Cook potatoes, covered, in boiling salted water in a large saucepan 15 minutes, or until tender; drain. Return potatoes to pan and shake over low heat until dry and fluffy. Place in a large bowl; drizzle oil-and-vinegar dressing over top. Let stand at least an hour to season.
2 Peel tomatoes, if you wish. Cut a thin slice from top of each, then scoop out insides with a teaspoon, being careful not to break shells. Turn tomato cups upside down on paper toweling to drain; chill.
3 Fold eggs, anchovies, olives, parsley and

All picnic portables (clockwise from top): Fruit Salad Palermo, Picnic Potato Cones, Mustard Bean Bowl.

chives into potato mixture; spoon into chilled tomato cups. Garnish each with two ripe olives threaded onto a wooden pick and serve on lettuce-lined plates, if you wish.

Note—Place tomato cups upright in a single layer in a flat pan; cover with foil. Carry potato mixture in a tightly covered bowl. Assemble salad at your eating spot.

Fruit Salad Palermo
Makes 8 servings

1½ cups uncooked ditalini macaroni or elbow
    spaghetti
  1 small ripe banana
½ cup mayonnaise or salad dressing
  1 tablespoon lemon juice

1 tablespoon honey
2 cups (1 pint) strawberries
3 medium-size seedless oranges
2 cups halved seedless green grapes

1 Cook macaroni or spaghetti in boiling salted water, following label directions; drain. Place in a large bowl; cool.
2 Mash banana in a small bowl; beat in mayonnaise or salad dressing, lemon juice and honey. Pour over macaroni; toss lightly to mix. Chill.
3 Just before serving, wash strawberries; hull and slice crosswise. Pare oranges and section. Arrange strawberries, orange sections and grape halves in rows on top of macaroni mixture; garnish edge of bowl with small romaine leaves, if you wish.
Note—To carry, pack fruits and macaroni with dressing in separate containers to assemble at serving time.

SWEETS TO PACK UP AND GO

Simple Savarin
Makes 12 servings

¾ cup sugar
Water
¼ cup light corn syrup
¼ cup dark rum
1 packaged lemon chiffon cake (17 ounces)
1 jar (10 ounces) apricot preserves
1 container (4½ ounces) frozen whipped topping, thawed
Chopped pecans

1 Combine sugar, ¾ cup water and corn syrup in a small saucepan. Heat, stirring constantly, to boiling, then cook rapidly 10 minutes; remove from heat. Cool 10 minutes; stir in rum.
2 Place cake on a deep platter; pierce all over with a long skewer. Drizzle part of the rum syrup over cake; let soak in, then repeat with remaining syrup until all has been absorbed. Chill cake.
3 Combine apricot preserves and 2 tablespoons water in a small saucepan; heat until bubbly; press through a sieve into a small bowl. Brush part over cake to coat evenly. Repeat until all apricot mixture has been used. Cool.
4 When ready to serve, spoon whipped topping into center of cake; sprinkle pecans over topping.
Note—Carry Savarin, whipped topping and nuts to picnic ground. Add topping and nuts just before serving.

Apricot Melba Tarts
Bake at 425° for 12 minutes. Makes 8 tarts

1 package piecrust mix
1 package (about 3 ounces) vanilla pudding and pie filling mix
1½ cups milk
1 package (8 ounces) cream cheese, cut up
1 can (about 1 pound) apricot halves, drained
Raspberry jelly

1 Prepare piecrust mix, following label directions; divide into 8 even pieces.
2 Roll out each on a lightly floured pastry cloth or board to a 5-inch circle; fit into a 3½-inch tart pan; trim edge flush with rim. Prick shells all over with a fork. Place in a large shallow pan for easy handling.
3 Bake in hot oven (425°) 12 minutes, or until golden. Cool completely in pans on wire racks.
4 Combine pudding mix, milk and cream cheese in a medium-size saucepan. Heat slowly, stirring constantly, until cheese melts, then cook, stirring constantly, until mixture thickens and bubbles 1 minute; remove from heat. Pour into a small bowl. Cool, stirring once or twice.
5 Spoon cream mixture into tart shells. Place 1 apricot half, cut side up, on top of each; spoon a rounded teaspoonful raspberry jelly into each hollow. Chill until serving time. (If serving tarts at home, remove shells from pans after they have cooled.)
Note—Leave tarts in pans for safe transit. Keep cool in an insulated tote bag until ready to serve.

Peanut Pops
Makes 8 servings

1 cup finely crushed peanut brittle
8 five-ounce paper cups
1 quart vanilla ice cream
8 tablespoons peanut butter
8 plastic spoons
8 squares foil

1 Spoon 1 tablespoon of the peanut brittle into each paper cup. Pack in part of the ice cream to half fill each; layer 1 tablespoon of the peanut butter, then remaining ice cream and peanut brittle on top. Pack down firmly with back of spoon.
2 Insert a plastic spoon, bowl end down, into each cup; wrap each in foil. Freeze until firm.
3 To serve, peel off foil and cups; eat ice cream from "stick." Or, leave cup in place, pull out spoon, and eat as an ice-cream sundae.
Note—Carry to picnic spot in insulated freezer chest.

All of these desserts are good travelers: Simple Savarin (left), Peanut Pops (top) and Apricot Melba Tarts.

Pineapple-Orange Deep-Dish Pie
Bake at 425° for 30 minutes. Makes 4 servings

3 large seedless oranges
1 can (1 pound, 4 ounces) pineapple chunks
 in pure juice
⅓ cup sugar (for filling)
3 tablespoons cornstarch
½ package piecrust mix

1 Pare oranges; section over a small bowl to catch the juice.
2 Drain juice from pineapple into a 1-cup measure; add the orange juice and water, if needed, to make ¾ cup.
3 Mix the ⅓ cup sugar and cornstarch in a medium-size saucepan; stir in the ¾ cup liquid. Cook over medium heat, stirring constantly, until sauce thickens and boils 3 minutes; re-

move from heat. Stir in pineapple chunks and orange sections; spoon into a deep 4-cup baking dish.

4 Prepare piecrust mix, following label directions. Roll out on a lightly floured pastry cloth or board to a circle 1 inch larger than baking dish; cut slits near center to let steam escape; place over filling in dish. Turn edge under, flush with rim of dish; flute edge.

5 Bake in hot oven (425°) 30 minutes, or until pastry is golden and juices bubble up. Cool on a wire rack. Spoon into serving dishes. Serve plain or with thawed frozen vanilla pudding.

Note—Steady casserole in a small box and carry to picnic ground.

Butterscotch Baked Apples
Bake at 350° for 50 minutes. Makes 6 servings

6 *medium-size baking apples*
½ *cup butterscotch sundae topping*
⅓ *cup brown-sugar-sweetened puffed rice cereal*
¼ *cup chopped walnuts*
1 *cup sugar*
¼ *cup water*

1 Core apples almost to bottom; pare about halfway down from stem end. Stand in a shallow baking dish, 13x9x2.

2 Mix butterscotch topping, cereal and walnuts in a small bowl; spoon into centers of apples.

3 Combine sugar and water in a small saucepan; heat to boiling; pour around apples.

4 Bake in moderate oven (350°), basting often with syrup in dish, 50 minutes, or until apples are tender but still firm enough to hold their shape. Cool, spooning syrup in dish over apples several times to make a rich glaze. Place in dessert dishes, adding a little of the extra syrup to each dish.

Note—Drain syrup from apples into a small screw-top jar. Carry apples to picnic site in their baking dish, well covered with foil. Syrup travels in its own jar.

Lime Fruit Bowl
Makes 6 servings

2 *eggs*
¼ *cup sugar*
2 *tablespoons butter or margarine*
½ *teaspoon grated lime peel*

Desserts "to go:" Choco-Banana Pops, Beach-Ball Cake.

3 tablespoons lime juice
¼ cup water
1 small ripe pineapple
1 ripe papaya
1 small honeydew melon
1 container (4½ ounces) frozen whipped topping, thawed

1 Beat eggs slightly in the top of a double boiler; stir in sugar, butter or margarine, lime peel and juice and water. Cook, stirring constantly, over simmering water, 10 minutes, or until very thick. Pour into a small bowl; cover. Chill until completely cold.
2 Pare pineapple; quarter lengthwise; core. Cut fruit into bite-size pieces. Pare papaya; halve lengthwise; scoop out seeds. Cube fruit. Halve melon; remove seeds. Cut into balls with a melon-ball cutter, or pare and cube. Combine fruits in a serving bowl; cover; chill.
3 Beat cream until stiff in a small bowl; fold into chilled lime mixture. Spoon fruit mixture into dessert dishes; spoon lime mixture over top.
Note—Carry mixed fruits to picnic ground in a large screw-top plastic container. Add cream at the very last minute.

Choco-Banana Pops
Children will enjoy these "lollipops" made of ripe bananas frosted with rich chocolate.
Makes 12 servings

1 package (6 ounces) semisweet-chocolate pieces
6 firm ripe bananas
12 long wooden skewers

1 Melt chocolate pieces in top of double boiler over simmering water; remove from heat but keep top over hot water.
2 Peel bananas, cut in half crosswise; insert a long wooden skewer into each. Holding each banana by its skewer "handle," frost with melted chocolate.
3 Place in single layer in buttered shallow pan; freeze 2 to 3 hours or until firm. Slip a fluted paper baking cup onto handle of each "lollipop" just before serving.
Note—Cover pops in pan with foil. Pack in a picnic cooler chest or insulated picnic bag.

Beach-Ball Cake
Make this fun cake for a party or to honor a young "beachcomber" on his birthday.
Bake at 325° for 55 minutes

Prepare 1 package of your favorite flavor angel-food cake mix, following label directions; pour batter into ungreased 12-cup ovenproof mixing bowl. Bake in slow oven (325°) 55 minutes, or until top is golden and a long, thin metal skewer inserted in center comes out clean. Turn cake upside down to cool, resting edge of bowl on three cans or glasses; cool completely. When cake has cooled, make FLUFFY FROSTING *(recipe follows)*. Loosen cake around edge of bowl with a knife; turn out, rounded side up, on wire rack. Mark cake into 6 wedge-shape sections with sharp point of knife; frost sections with alternating white and yellow FLUFFY FROSTING. Tint 1⅓ cups flaked coconut (3½-ounce can) yellow by shaking with ¼ teaspoon water and a few drops yellow food coloring in a jar with tight-fitting cover; sprinkle over yellow sections. Sprinkle 1⅓ cups (3½-ounce can) plain flaked coconut over white sections. Decorate top with a candy-peppermint-patty "button" fastened with a dot of frosting. Makes 12 servings.

FLUFFY FROSTING—Combine 2 unbeaten egg whites and ¼ teaspoon cream of tartar in medium-size bowl; beat with rotary beater or electric mixer until egg whites stand in firm peaks. Combine 2 tablespoons light corn syrup, 2½ tablespoons water and 1½ teaspoons vanilla in a cup; add alternately with 4 cups (1 pound) sifted 10X (confectioners' powdered) sugar to egg-white mixture, beating well after each addition, until frosting is creamy-stiff. Spoon half into second bowl and tint yellow with a few drops yellow food coloring; leave remaining half white. Makes enough to frost one 12-cup-bowl cake.
Note—Place cake in a box or plastic-dome cake carrier (top fastens securely to bottom). Take along a cake knife and paper plates.

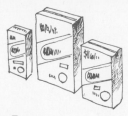

Watermelon Fancy
You can't find a more popular, easier-to-fix picnic dessert.

Buy a ripe whole watermelon (it will give a dull thumping sound when tapped). Cut off a slice across the top equal to ⅓ of the melon; lift off. For a party touch, make even saw-tooth cuts into rind of larger piece all the way around. Run knife around inside of rind to loosen melon from edge about 3 inches down; cut fruit down middle, then slice crosswise into thick pieces; pry out pieces with tip of knife. Cut sections from

1397

"lid" of melon the same way; pile all back into melon shell. Chill until serving time. Serve plain or with a sprinkling of salt.
Note—Cover with transparent wrap or foil and set in a sturdy cardboard box or basket.

STURDY COOKIE TRAVELERS

Note—Pack each kind separately in plastic sandwich boxes or wrap, two by two, back to back, in wax paper or transparent wrap and tote in a small cardboard box, cushioning, as needed, with wads of wax paper.

Apple Saucers
Golden circles, nice and spicy, munchy with walnuts and currants.
Bake at 350° for 15 minutes. Makes 1½ dozen 4-inch cookies

    2 cups sifted all-purpose flour
    1 teaspoon baking powder
    1 teaspoon pumpkin-pie spice
    ½ teaspoon baking soda
    ½ teaspoon salt
    ½ cup (1 stick) butter or margarine
    1 cup firmly packed brown sugar
    1 egg
    1 teaspoon vanilla
    1 cup canned applesauce
    1 cup currants
    1 cup coarsely broken walnuts

1 Measure flour, baking powder, spice, soda and salt into sifter.
2 Cream butter or margarine with brown sugar until fluffy in a large bowl; beat in egg and vanilla. Sift in flour mixture, adding alternately with applesauce; blend well; stir in currants and nuts.
3 Drop dough, ¼ cupful at a time, 6 inches apart, on greased large cookie sheets; spread into 3-inch rounds.
4 Bake in moderate oven (350°) 15 minutes, or until lightly browned around edges. Remove cookies to wire racks to cool. Leave plain, or sprinkle with 10X (confectioners' powdered) sugar.

1398

Chocolate-Mint Blossoms
Flowers start as separate petals of dough, "grow" together in baking.

Bake at 350° for 10 minutes. Makes 1½ dozen 4-inch cookies

    2 cups sifted all-purpose flour
    ⅓ cup cocoa (not a mix)
    1½ teaspoons baking powder
    ½ teaspoon salt
    1¼ cups vegetable shortening
    1 cup sugar
    2 eggs
    ½ teaspoon peppermint extract

1 Measure flour, cocoa, baking powder and salt into sifter.
2 Cream shortening with sugar until fluffy in a large bowl; beat in eggs and peppermint extract. Sift in flour mixture, blending well. Chill until firm enough to handle.
3 Roll dough, a heaping teaspoonful at a time, into 1½-inch-long ovals; place in groups of 4, pinwheel fashion, 3 inches apart, on greased large cookie sheets; flatten to ⅛ inch thickness.
4 Bake in moderate oven (350°) 10 minutes, or until firm. Remove cookies to wire racks to cool. Decorate with pink frosting from a pressurized can and crushed peppermint candy, if you wish.

Orange Sugar Squares
New angle on sugar cookies—the flavor of orange. Frost or not, as you like.
Bake at 400° for 8 minutes. Makes sixteen 4-inch cookies

    2½ cups sifted all-purpose flour
    2 teaspoons baking powder
    1 teaspoon salt
    ¾ cup (1½ sticks) butter or margarine
    1¼ cups sugar
    2 eggs
    1 tablespoon grated orange peel

1 Measure flour, baking powder and salt into sifter.
2 Cream butter or margarine with 1 cup of the sugar until fluffy in a large bowl; beat in eggs and orange peel. Sift in flour mixture, ⅓ at a time, blending well. Chill until firm enough to handle.
3 Roll out dough to a 16-inch square on a lightly floured pastry cloth or board; sprinkle with remaining ¼ cup sugar. Cut into 4-inch squares. Place, 1 inch apart, on large cookie sheets.

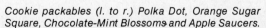

Cookie packables (l. to r.) Polka Dot, Orange Sugar Square, Chocolate-Mint Blossoms and Apple Saucers.

4 Bake in hot oven (400°) 8 minutes, or until firm. Remove cookies to wire racks to cool. Leave plain, or drizzle with your favorite orange frosting, if you wish.

Lemon Crinkles

These lemony wafers crinkle prettily as they bake with a sparkle of sugar on top.
Bake at 350° for 8 to 10 minutes. Makes about 5 dozen

    ¾ cup butter or margarine
    1¼ cups sugar
    1 egg
    ½ teaspoon vanilla
    ½ teaspoon lemon extract
    ¼ cup milk
    2 cups sifted all-purpose flour
    1 teaspoon baking powder
    ½ teaspoon salt
    ¼ teaspoon baking soda
    1 tablespoon grated lemon peel

1 Cream butter or margarine with ¾ cup sugar until light in medium-size bowl (save remaining ½ cup for Step 3). Beat in egg, vanilla, lemon extract and milk.
2 Sift in flour, baking powder, salt and baking soda, a little at a time, blending after each addition; chill dough several hours, or until firm.
3 Form into marble-size balls (about 1 teaspoonful for each) by rolling lightly between palms of hands. Coat balls by rolling in a mixture of saved ½ cup sugar and lemon peel; place 2 inches apart on ungreased cookie sheets.
4 Bake in moderate oven (350°) 8 to 10 minutes, or until tops are crackled and edges are lightly browned; cool completely on wire racks.

1400

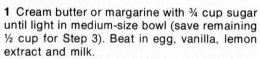

Spicy Hermits

The big-hit cookie, made doubly rich with nut-flavor wheat germ.
Bake at 375° for 10 minutes. Makes about 2 dozen

    1¾ cups sifted all-purpose flour
    ½ teaspoon salt
    ½ teaspoon baking soda

    ½ teaspoon ground nutmeg
    ½ teaspoon ground cinnamon
    ¼ teaspoon ground cloves
    ½ cup (1 stick) butter or margarine
    1 cup firmly packed brown sugar
    1 egg
    ¼ cup cold brewed coffee
    ½ cup wheat germ (from a 12-ounce jar)
    1 cup seedless raisins
    ½ cup coarsely chopped walnuts

1 Measure flour, salt, baking soda, nutmeg, cinnamon and cloves into sifter.
2 Cream butter or margarine with sugar until fluffy in medium-size bowl; beat in egg. Sift in dry ingredients, a third at a time, adding alternately with coffee; stir in remaining ingredients.
3 Drop by rounded teaspoonfuls, about 2 inches apart, on greased cookie sheets.
4 Bake in moderate oven (375°) 10 minutes, or until firm. Remove from cookie sheets; cool completely on racks.

Mint Puffs

Bake at 375° for 12 minutes. Makes 2 dozen cookies

    1 package chocolate-mint cookie mix
    ½ cup dairy sour cream
    1 egg
    1 cup cocoa-sweetened toasted rice cereal
      (from a 9-ounce package)

1 Combine cookie mix, sour cream and egg in a medium-size bowl; beat until well blended. Stir in chocolate pieces (from cookie mix package) and cereal.
2 Drop dough by rounded tablespoonfuls onto lightly greased cookie sheets.
3 Bake in moderate oven (375°) 12 minutes, or until centers are firm. Cool on cookie sheets 1 minute; remove to wire racks. Cool completely.

Polka Dots

Tiny marshmallows dot butterscotch rounds, bake just long enough to melt.
Bake at 375° for 12 minutes. Makes 1½ dozen 4-inch cookies

    2¼ cups sifted all-purpose flour
    ¾ teaspoon baking soda
    ½ teaspoon salt

1 cup (2 sticks) butter or margarine
1 cup firmly packed dark brown sugar
½ cup granulated sugar
2 eggs
1½ teaspoons vanilla
1 package (6 ounces) butterscotch-flavor pieces
1 cup tiny marshmallows

1 Measure flour, soda and salt into sifter.
2 Cream butter or margarine with sugars until fluffy in a large bowl; beat in eggs and vanilla. Sift in flour mixture, ⅓ at a time, blending well; stir in butterscotch pieces.
3 Drop dough, a scant ¼ cupful at a time, 6 inches apart, on large cookie sheets; spread into 4-inch rounds.
4 Bake in moderate oven (375°) 10 minutes; place several marshmallows on top of each cookie. Bake 1 to 2 minutes longer, or just until marshmallows melt. Remove to wire racks to cool.

Milk-Chocolate Marble Bars
Bake at 350° for 45 minutes. Makes 24 bars

3 cups biscuit mix
1 cup sugar
2 eggs
8 tablespoons (1 stick) butter or margarine, softened
1 cup milk
1 tablespoon vanilla
2 envelopes (1 ounce each) liquid unsweetened chocolate
1 package creamy milk-chocolate frosting mix
¼ cup lukewarm water
1 cup pecan halves
1 cup tiny marshmallows

1 Combine biscuit mix, sugar, eggs, 4 tablespoons of the butter or margarine, milk and vanilla in a large bowl. Beat at low speed with an electric mixer until blended, then beat at medium speed, scraping bowl several times, 4 minutes. Or beat vigorously 2 minutes by hand.
2 Spread half the batter in a greased-and-floured baking pan, 13x9x2.
3 Stir chocolate into remaining batter in bowl; drop by spoonfuls onto batter in pan; draw a knife through batters several times to marble.
4 Bake in moderate oven (350°) 45 minutes, or until top springs back when lightly pressed with fingertip. Cool in pan on a wire rack.

5 Combine frosting mix, lukewarm water and remaining 4 tablespoons butter or margarine in a medium-size bowl; beat, following label directions. Fold in pecans and marshmallows; spread over cake. Let stand until frosting is firm. Cut into quarters, then cut each quarter into 6 bars. *Note*—Carry in baking pan, uncut, and cut into bars at the picnic.

Oatmeal Spice Squares
Bake at 375° for 35 minutes. Makes 24 squares

1¾ cups sifted all-purpose flour
1½ teaspoons baking soda
¾ teaspoon ground cinnamon
¼ teaspoon ground cloves
¼ teaspoon ground nutmeg
½ cup (1 stick) butter or margarine
1 cup firmly packed light brown sugar
2 eggs
1 teaspoon vanilla
1 cup applesauce
1½ cups quick-cooking rolled oats
1 package (8 ounces) pitted dates, finely chopped
½ cup chopped walnuts
CITRUS GLAZE (recipe follows)

1 Sift flour, soda, cinnamon, cloves and nutmeg onto wax paper.
2 Cream butter or margarine with brown sugar until fluffy in a large bowl; beat in eggs, one at a time, and vanilla. Stir in flour mixture, half at a time, alternately with applesauce, just until blended; stir in rolled oats, dates and walnuts. Spoon into a greased pan, 13x9x2; spread top even.
3 Bake in moderate oven (375°) 35 minutes, or until center springs back when lightly pressed with fingertip. Cool completely in pan on a wire rack.
4 Drizzle CITRUS GLAZE over top; let stand until firm. Cut into serving-size squares.

CITRUS GLAZE—Blend ½ cup 10X (confectioners' powdered) sugar with 2 teaspoons water and 2 teaspoons lemon juice until smooth in a small bowl.
Note—Carry in baking pan, uncut, and cut into bars at the picnic.

1401

NUTS

NUTS

NUTS:
TIPS ON BUYING AND STORING NUTS, HOW TO PREPARE THEM, BASIC RECIPES, HOW TO USE FRESH COCONUTS

Nuts—every nibbler's favorite, every dieter's nemesis (nuts *do* run to calories, alas, but unlike many other high-calorie foods, they are also jam-packed with nutritive value).

Nuts are many a party's mainstay, many a recipe's magic ingredient. Most candies are made better with nuts, many cakes and cookies, even soups and salads, seafood, meats and vegetables.

A scatter of toasty brown almond slivers atop a butter-broiled fillet of sole is a classic; so, too, is a torte made of ground walnuts, a soup of pulverized peanuts, a pie studded with plump pecan halves (these recipes will be found in other volumes of THE FAMILY CIRCLE ILLUSTRATED LIBRARY OF COOKING). What we concentrate upon here are the basics—the *nuts* and bolts, so to speak. There are shopping and storage tips, directions for blanching, chopping, grating, slivering and toasting nuts, plus recipes for such cocktail party favorites as butter-roasted nuts, garlic and smoky-flavored nuts. In addition, there are recipes for candies, confections and cookies that owe their special goodness to nuts.

Facts about Nuts:
Whatever your need—nuts in the shell or out; in transparent bags, vacuum bags, cans or glass jars; in halves, pieces or chopped—your supermarket has them. Nuts in the shell are usually displayed in the produce department; cans, jars and bags, with the baking supplies or in the candy section. You'll find a wide range of package sizes to fit every recipe need.

You Can Afford to Be Choosy:
Most popular for cooking and snacks are walnuts, almonds, pecans, peanuts, filberts or hazelnuts, cashews, pistachios, black walnuts, Brazil nuts and hickory nuts—and most can be used interchangeably. One cup of nuts you shell at home may cost less than a can or bag of ready-to-use ones, but to get the most for your money, your time should be counted, too. In shelled varieties, buy according to your need. For example: Chopped or pieces—usually lower in price—are perfect for stirring into cookies or candy; whole or halves, for garnishing or decorating. Knowing how many to buy is important, and this handy chart will guide you on how the most popular kinds measure up.

In shell		When shelled
Walnuts,	1 pound	2 cups
Almonds,	1 pound	2 cups
Pecans,	1 pound	2¼ cups
Peanuts,	1 pound	2 cups
Filberts,	1 pound	1½ cups

Shelled		Measure
Walnuts,	4 ounces	1 cup
Almonds,	5 ounces	1 cup
Pecans,	3 ounces	1 cup
Peanuts,	7 ounces	1½ cups
Filberts,	4 ounces	1 cup

What Does "Dry-Roasted" or "Dry-Toasted" Mean?
Some jar-packed peanuts, cashews, mixed nuts and almonds carry either description, which simply means that the nuts have been processed with no fat, oil or sugar added, and have fewer calories. To illustrate the comparison: A handful of ordinary peanuts—or about 18—is 171 calories, whereas the same amount of dry-roasted or dry-toasted ones is 56 calories.

Storage Tips:
Nuts are one of the easiest of all foods to store, so it's no problem to have them on hand. In the shell they stay fresh if kept in a cool, dark place. Once cans or packages of shelled varieties are opened, recap or reseal and store in the refrigerator. Or place in a plastic bag, seal and freeze. Either way, they'll stay fresh and crisp for several months.

SOME NUT PREPARATION TIPS

• *How to Blanch:* Almonds and peanuts both have, in addition to their shells, tightly clinging brown or reddish skins. For most recipes, the nuts must be blanched ("skinned"). The best way is to immerse the nuts in boiling water, dropping them into the water gradually so that the boiling doesn't stop, then to let them boil for about a minute. Drain the nuts, then slip off the skins with your fingers.

• *How to Chop Nuts:* The most efficient way is with a heavy French chopping knife. Place a small mound of nuts on a chopping block or board, then chop back and forth in an arc until they're the desired degree of fineness. Blenders can be used for chopping but they work so fast that they may overchop the nuts.

• *How to Grate Nuts:* If the nuts are to be grated very fine, use an electric blender. Do only about a cup of nuts at a time, stopping and stirring up from the bottom as needed to keep nuts from clumping. For more coarsely grated nuts, use the handy little rotary grater.

• *How to Sliver Almonds:* It's easier than you think. All you have to do is to peel off strips with a vegetable parer while the almonds are still damp from blanching.

Butter-Roasted Nuts
Roast at 300° for 40 to 45 minutes. Makes 1 pound

1 pound shelled pecans or walnuts or 1 pound shelled and blanched almonds or peanuts
1 tablespoon butter or margarine
½ teaspoon salt

1 Place nuts in a single layer in a large shallow baking pan, roast in a very slow oven (300°), shaking pan or stirring nuts often, for 20 to 30 minutes or until beginning to turn golden.
2 Dot with butter or margarine, shake nuts in pan to coat well and continue roasting, shaking once or twice, 10 to 15 minutes longer or until crisp and richly golden. Sprinkle with salt.

Piquant Roasted Nuts: Roast as directed but sprinkle with seasoned salt instead of plain salt.

Garlic-Roasted Nuts: Roast as directed but sprinkle with garlic salt instead of plain salt.

Onion-Roasted Nuts: Roast as directed but sprinkle with onion salt instead of plain salt.

Smoky Roasted Nuts: Roast as directed but sprinkle with hickory-flavor salt instead of plain salt.

Edenton Fried Peanuts
Edenton is the capital of North Carolina's peanut country and this is the favorite Edenton way of cooking raw peanuts.
Makes 1 pound

1 pound shelled and blanched raw peanuts
Peanut oil or vegetable oil for deep fat frying
Salt

1 Make sure peanuts are thoroughly dry after they have been blanched.
2 Heat peanut oil or vegetable oil in a deep fat fryer to 300°. Add peanuts and fry, stirring constantly, until pale golden (they will continue cooking after they're removed from the deep fat so it's best to pull them out when they are just *faintly* brown).
3 Drain on several thicknesses of paper toweling; sprinkle with salt; cool. Store in a covered container.

Curried Nuts
Makes 1 pound

2 tablespoons + 2 teaspoons butter or margarine
1 tablespoon curry powder
1 pound pecan or walnut halves or 1 pound whole shelled and blanched almonds
¼ teaspoon salt

1 Melt butter or margarine in a very large frying pan; stir in curry powder and cook slowly 5 minutes.
2 Stir in nuts and heat very slowly, stirring often, 5 to 8 minutes or until lightly toasted. Cool on paper toweling, tossing to drain off excess butter. Sprinkle with salt, toss again. Store in a tightly covered container.

Chili Nuts: Prepare as directed but substitute 1 tablespoon chili powder for the curry powder.

1403

Mexicali Almonds
Bake at 350° for 25 minutes. Makes about 2 cups

1 tablespoon butter or margarine
2 cans (5 ounces each) whole blanched almonds
1 teaspoon chili powder
1 teaspoon garlic salt

1 Melt butter or margarine in a shallow baking pan; stir in almonds.
2 Bake in moderate oven (350°) 15 minutes, or until toasted.
3 Sprinkle with chili powder and garlic salt; toss to coat almonds.
4 Bake 10 minutes longer. Spread almonds on paper toweling to cool. Store in a tightly covered container.

SOME NUT-TY SWEETS AND SWEETMEATS

Spiced Walnuts
Bake at 325° for 30 minutes. Makes 1 pound

1 pound shelled walnuts (halves or pieces)
1 tablespoon butter or margarine
1 teaspoon cinnamon-sugar

1 Place walnuts in a large saucepan, cover with boiling water and heat 3 minutes; drain well.
2 Spread nuts in a single layer in a shallow baking pan. Bake in a slow oven (325°), shaking pan often, 30 minutes or until crisp and richly browned.
3 Add butter or margarine and toss to coat well. Sprinkle with cinnamon-sugar and cool. Store in a covered container.

Spiced Pecans: Substitute pecan halves for the walnuts. Do not boil but spread in a single layer in a shallow baking pan. Roast and season as directed.

Pecan Crunch
Makes 4 cups

2 tablespoons butter or margarine
2 teaspoons cinnamon-sugar

1 can (6 ounces) pecan halves
2 cups sugar-and-honey-sweetened corn cereal (from a 5-ounce package)

1 Melt butter or margarine in a large frying pan; stir in remaining ingredients and toss lightly to mix.
2 Heat very slowly, stirring often, 5 minutes or until lightly toasted; cool. Store in a tightly covered container.

Pecan Brittle
Makes about 2½ pounds

5 cups unsalted pecan halves
2 cups sugar
1 cup light corn syrup
¼ cup water
2 tablespoons butter or margarine
2 teaspoons baking soda
1 tablespoon orange extract

1 Butter a baking pan, 15x10x1; spread nuts evenly in pan.
2 Combine sugar, corn syrup and water in a kettle. Heat slowly, stirring constantly, until sugar dissolves, then cook, without stirring, to 280° on a candy thermometer. Stir in butter or margarine; cook to 300°; remove from heat.
3 Stir in soda and orange extract. (Mixture will foam.) Drizzle quickly over nuts in pan to cover evenly. Let stand until firm. Break into bite-size pieces. Store in a tightly covered container.

Almond-Raisin Mixup
Slightly salty, and one nibble just invites you to have another.
Bake at 300° for 20 minutes. Makes 5 cups

Melt 4 teaspoons butter or margarine in a large shallow baking pan; stir in 2 cans (5 ounces each) whole blanched almonds. Bake in slow oven (300°), stirring often, 20 minutes, or until almonds are lightly toasted; remove from oven. Stir in 1 package (15 ounces) golden raisins and ⅛ teaspoon salt; toss lightly to mix; cool. Store in a tightly covered container.

Minted Glazed Pecans
They're really luscious—a wonderful combination of flavors.
Makes about 3 cups

1 cup sugar
¼ cup light corn syrup

½ cup water
1 cup tiny marshmallows
½ teaspoon essence of peppermint
1 pound (about 3 cups) shelled pecans

1 Heat sugar, corn syrup and water in saucepan; stir until syrup begins to boil, then cook to 238° on a candy thermometer (a teaspoonful of syrup dropped into cold water will form a soft ball).
2 Remove from heat; quickly stir in and melt marshmallows; add peppermint and pecans; stir to coat nuts well.
3 Pour onto wax paper or foil; separate while still warm; cool until glaze is hardened. Store in airtight container.

Nut Sparkles
Nuts spiced as our Mexican neighbors like 'em. Be prepared for recipe requests.
Makes 2 cups

1 egg white
½ cup sugar
1 tablespoon instant coffee powder
¼ teaspoon salt
¼ teaspoon ground cinnamon
2 cups mixed shelled nuts (walnuts, pecans, Brazil nuts, filberts, blanched almonds, Macadamia nuts or peanuts)

1 Beat egg white until foamy in medium-size bowl; blend in sugar, instant coffee, salt and cinnamon.
2 Stir in nuts and coat well; lift out, a few at a time, with fork; hold over bowl to drain; place, without touching one another, on buttered cookie sheet.
3 Toast in slow oven (325°) about 20 minutes, or until golden.
4 Cool and store in airtight container.

Spiced-Nut Clusters
Perfect as a gift—or served at your own open house.
Bake at 325° about 20 minutes. Makes about 3 dozen

1 egg white
½ cup sugar
1 teaspoon salt
1 teaspoon ground cinnamon
¼ teaspoon ground nutmeg
¼ teaspoon ground cloves
½ cup walnut halves

½ cup pecan halves
½ cup blanched almonds
½ cup shelled filberts

1 Beat egg white until foamy in medium-size bowl; blend in sugar, salt, cinnamon, nutmeg and cloves.
2 Add nuts; stir until well coated.
3 Lift out nuts, a few at a time, with fork; hold over bowl to drain; place in clusters on buttered cookie sheet.
4 Bake in slow oven (325°) about 20 minutes, or until golden.
5 Remove at once from cookie sheet with spatula; cool on wire cake rack.

Nut Nuggets
Bake at 350° for 12 to 15 minutes. Makes about 6 dozen cookies

1 cup (2 sticks) butter or margarine
½ cup brown sugar, firmly packed
1 egg yolk
2 cups sifted all-purpose flour
1 egg white, slightly beaten
1 cup unblanched pistachio nuts, finely chopped

1 Cream butter or margarine with brown sugar until light and fluffy in bowl; beat in egg yolk; stir in flour.
2 Form into marble-size balls by rolling between palms of hands; dip each in egg white; roll in nuts; place on ungreased cookie sheets.
3 Bake in moderate oven (350°) 12 to 15 minutes, or until firm when lightly pressed with fingertip.

Cafe-Cream Nuts
Makes about 2½ pounds

1 cup firmly packed light brown sugar
½ cup granulated sugar
1 tablespoon instant coffee powder
¼ teaspoon ground cinnamon
½ cup dairy sour cream
1 teaspoon vanilla
3 cups mixed shelled nuts (walnuts, pecans, Brazil nuts, almonds)

1 Combine sugars, coffee, cinnamon and sour cream in medium-size saucepan; cook, without stirring, over medium heat to 238° on a candy thermometer or until a teaspoon of mixture dropped in cold water forms a soft ball.
2 Remove from heat; stir in vanilla and nuts.

1405

3 Spread thinly on a buttered cookie sheet. Cool and separate into bite-size pieces.

Pistachio Ripple Cakes

Grated chocolate and chopped nuts twirl all the way through these little spongelike butter-cake sweets.
Bake at 350° for 30 minutes. Makes 36 tiny cakes

½ cup (1 stick) butter or margarine
3 eggs
1½ cups granulated sugar
½ teaspoon vanilla
¼ teaspoon almond extract
1 cup sifted cake flour
¼ cup finely chopped pistachio nuts
½ square semisweet chocolate, grated
10X (confectioners' powdered) sugar
VANILLA-ALMOND CREAM (recipe follows)
Pistachio nuts, quartered

1 Grease and lightly flour a baking pan, 9x9x2.
2 Melt butter or margarine in a small saucepan; cool.
3 Beat eggs until foamy in large bowl of electric mixer; beat in granulated sugar, 1 tablespoon at a time, beating all the time until mixture is fluffy-light and triple in volume. (Beating will take about 15 minutes in all.) Beat in vanilla and almond extract.
4 Fold in flour, alternately with cooled butter or margarine, until no streaks of flour remain.
5 Pour half of batter into prepared pan; sprinkle with half of the chopped nuts and grated chocolate. Pour remaining batter over; sprinkle with remaining nuts and chocolate. Cut through batter with a knife to swirl nuts and chocolate and make a marble effect.
6 Bake in moderate oven (350°) 30 minutes, or until cake pulls away from sides of pan and top springs back when lightly pressed with fingertip. Cool on wire rack 5 minutes; turn out onto rack; cool completely.
7 Cut into 36 small squares. Sprinkle with sifted 10X sugar; top each with a rosette of VANILLA-ALMOND CREAM put through a cake-decorating set. Garnish with quartered pistachio nuts.

VANILLA-ALMOND CREAM—Beat 3 tablespoons softened butter or margarine with ¾ cup sifted 10X (confectioner's powdered) sugar, a dash of salt, 1 teaspoon milk, ½ teaspoon vanilla and ¼ teaspoon almond extract in a small bowl until creamy-smooth. Makes about ½ cup.

1406

FRESH COCONUT NIBBLES

Sample one of these golden crispies and you'll go back for a handful—they're that good! If fixing a coconut has always baffled you, the steps below show you that it's easier than it seems. Sweet and tangy seasoners are suggested here, but salty ones are equally tempting.

Open a fresh coconut this way:
1 Drain Milk—Look for the three "eyes" at one end of the coconut and puncture each with an ice pick or punch and hammers. Then hold the nut over a bowl until all of the milk drains away. Chill milk to enjoy as a beverage or spoon over vanilla custard.
2 Crack Shell—Again, the hammer is your handiest tool, and you'll find it easiest to work on a firm surface such as a cutting board or even outdoors on a flat stone. Or crack shell in a vise. You'll be amazed how easily the brown woody shell falls away in big chunks, leaving pieces of the white nut covered with a wrinkly brown skin.
3 Remove Skin—Work with big or little pieces of the coconut, whichever are easiest for you to handle, and, using your trusty vegetable parer, shave off brown covering.
4 Make Curls—Shave the moist nut into paper-thin strips. A vegetable parer speeds the job, but you can use a sharp thin-blade knife if you prefer. Spread strips in a layer in a large shallow baking pan.
5 Toast Strips—Bake in very slow oven (275°), turning them often, 45 minutes, or until dry, slightly curled, and toasty-golden. Use plain as a garnish for cakes, pies, pudding desserts, or curry. For snacktime nibbles, season with table salt or one of the flavor extras given below. A medium-size coconut will make about four cups of chips. To keep them crisp, store in a tightly covered container.

Orange-Coconut Chips:
Sprinkle 1 teaspoon grated orange peel over toasted chips while they're still warm; toss gently to mix. Cool completely before storing.

Sugar-and-Spice Chips:
Sprinkle 2 teaspoons cinnamon-sugar over toasted chips while they're still warm; toss gently to mix. Cool completely before storing.

INDEX TO RECIPES IN THIS VOLUME